CONTENTS

Part 1   The Jewish faith

Part 2 Christianity

MICHAEL
KEENE

BELIEVERS

IN

ONE GOD

Judaism

Christianity

Islam

CAMBRIDGE
UNIVERSITY PRESS

Published by the Press Syndicate of the University of Cambridge
The Pitt Building, Trumpington Street, Cambridge CB2 1RP
40 West 20th Street, New York, NY 10011-4211, USA
10 Stamford Road, Oakleigh, Victoria 3166, Australia

© Cambridge University Press 1993
First published 1993
Reprinted with corrections 1995
Printed in Great Britain at the University Press, Cambridge
A catalogue record for this book is available from the British Library
ISBN 0 521 38627 6 paperback
Project editors: Elizabeth Paren and Gill Stacey
Picture research: Angela Anderson
Cover and interior design by Design / Section
Map illustrations by Lorraine Harrison

ACKNOWLEDGEMENTS

The publishers would like to thank the following for their
permission to include copyright photographs: Andes Press
Agency/Carlos Reyes, pp. 36 (top), 60, 98, 101 (both); Angela
Anderson, pp. 26 (right), 159; Barnaby's Picture Library, pp. 16, 95,
157; Camera Press/Michael Charity, p. 87; Chris Fairclough Colour
Library, pp. 35, 109; Daisy Hayes, p. 110; Douglas Hollidge, p. 112;
Liverpool Cathedral, p. 93; Methodist Church Overseas Division,
pp. 74 (Gordon Shaw), 106 (Jenny Matthews); Christine Osborne
Pictures, pp. 53, 71, 73, 131, 134, 144, 151, 167; Out-Take, pp. 20,
54; Popperfoto, pp. 15, 68, 77; Zev Radovan, pp. 23, 31, 39; Rex
Features, pp. 6, 47, 63, 127, 166; Peter Sanders, pp. 121, 129, 133,
139, 146, 149, 153, 160, 162, 165, 173; Juliette Soester, pp. 26 (left),
33, 36 (bottom), 41, 43, 44, 57; Tate Gallery, p. 82; Topham Picture
Source, p. 116; Geoff Ward, pp. 79, 85, 91 (both), 103; Wiener
Library, p. 18; Zefa Picture Library, pp. 48, 95.

Part 3 Islam

PART 1

THE JEWISH FAITH

1. THE JEWS IN HISTORY

1.1 Being a Jew

Focusing questions
- How old is the Jewish religion?
- What or who is a Jew?
- What links does a Jew today feel with the past?

A Jewish father and child in Tel Aviv, Israel. Make sure you know where Israel is.

The history of the Jewish people began at least 4,000 years ago when a group of people, called the **Israelites**, lived in the small country of **Israel**. This tribe, also known for a time as **Hebrews**, developed a language of their own (**Hebrew**) in which their scriptures were written. **Jews** today are the direct spiritual descendants of these ancient Israelites and, as such, they belong to one of the world's oldest surviving religions.

Numerically **Judaism** is also one of the world's smallest religions – there are just about 15,000,000 Jews worldwide. Some 30 per cent of this number live in the USA and 25 per cent in Israel. Britain has a large Jewish community with about 385,000 members. Thousands more live in the USSR and other European countries.

What it means to be a Jew

Although for most of their history Jews have been dispersed throughout the world, there have always been very close links between the different Jewish communities.

Ever since God first 'spoke' to Abraham (see 1.2) the Israelites, and later the Jews, have believed that they are part of a unique religious faith. Anyone who has a Jewish mother is automatically part of that faith. Even though many Jews today do not practise that faith (these people are known as secular Jews) they cannot turn their backs on their Jewish heritage altogether. They remain Jewish.

Being a Jew means sharing and celebrating rituals, food laws, festivals and songs with others. This sharing with one another is a very important part of what it means to be Jewish.

Although a non-Jewish person (a **Gentile**) can be converted to the faith this would be very unusual. The vast majority of Jews are born into the faith and since this has always been the case Jews today feel a very close link with the ancient Israelites and Jewish people down the centuries. These close links between living Jews and Jews long dead have led many people to talk of the 'Jewish family'.

As you will discover, the Jewish religion is all about living. Being a Jew means adopting a certain way of life and living by the standards that God has laid down in the Holy Scriptures.

Key question   **What is distinctive about being a Jew?**

Work to do

Two young people are talking about their Jewish background and what it means to them today:

☐ *I was always taught to believe that anyone who has a Jewish mother is a Jew. What's more, I cannot discard my Jewishness like an old coat. Once a Jew always a Jew. I am a Jew. Yet I do not carry out most of the traditional Jewish practices. I do not go to the synagogue on shabat, I do not celebrate the Jewish festivals and I do not pray. Yet I am still a Jew.*

☐ *My Jewish faith means a great deal to me. I was circumcised as a baby, I became bar mitzvah on my 13th birthday, I married a Jewish woman and I am bringing up my family in the Jewish way of life.*

(a) What word would describe the kind of Jewess speaking in 1?

(b) Why do you think that a person is proud to be known as a Jew even though they do not follow any of the Jewish religious practices?

(c) How important are the various religious customs to the man speaking in 2?

Key words   **Gentile:** originally someone who was not an Israelite; now the term refers to anyone who is not a Jew

Hebrew: member of one of the tribes which eventually became the people of Israel; also the language of this people, and of the modern state of Israel

Israel: country occupied by Hebrews (Israelites)

Israelites: another name for Hebrews – according to Genesis the Israelites were the descendants of Jacob, who was also known as Israel

Jews: spiritual and actual descendants of the ancient Israelites – the term derives from the word 'Judah', the name of one of the original tribes of Israel

Judaism: religion of the Jews

1.2 The beginning of the Jewish nation

Focusing questions

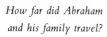

■ How does the Jewish Bible start?
■ What change came over Abraham whilst he lived in Ur of the Chaldees?
■ Who were the patriarchs?

How far did Abraham and his family travel?

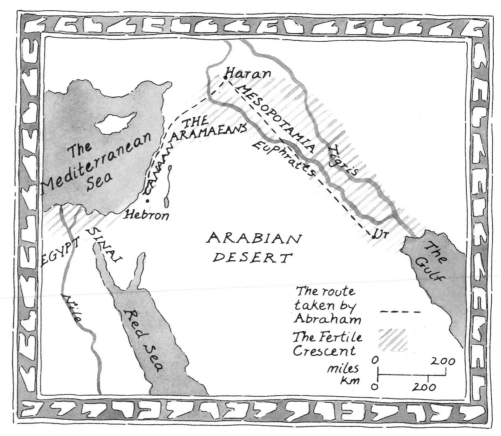

The **Jewish Bible** opens with two descriptions of the creation of the world: the story of how the first man and woman disobeyed God, and an account of how God sent a flood to destroy all living things. It is only after this material has been covered that we learn just how the Jewish nation began. The Bible informs us that it started with **Abraham**.

Abraham

Abram, or Abraham as he was later called, was brought up in the small town of Ur of the Chaldees. There, along with everyone else, he worshipped the many gods who were believed to have control over different parts of nature. Then Abraham encountered the one God who seemed to control not only the whole of nature but history as well. This same God was willing to enter into a special agreement (covenant) with Abraham and his descendants.

No one is quite sure just how, or when, Abraham stopped believing in many gods and came to believe in one God. The time and the place, though, are not important. What matters is that Abraham's experience marked the beginning of the Jewish nation, and Jews today speak, with great fondness, of 'our father, Abraham' (Avraham Avinu).

Although this experience cannot be dated precisely it seems to have taken place some time between 2000 **BCE** and 1800 BCE. The outcome of it was that Abraham uprooted his extensive family from the town of Ur of the Chaldees and took them 500 miles away to Haran. From there they travelled a further 500 miles to Canaan, where God revealed to Abraham that his descendants would be protected and would, in time, grow into a great nation.

The patriarchs

Because the Jewish nation grew out of the descendants of Abraham he is often referred to as one of the **patriarchs** (father-figures) of that nation. The other two patriarchs were **Isaac**, Abraham's son, and his son **Jacob**. According to the **Torah** God commanded Abraham to offer Isaac as a sacrifice but spared him at the last moment. Jacob was also called Israel, a name which tells us that he was the founding father of one of the 12 tribes of the 'chosen people' of the Israelites (the 'Children of Israel').

As semi-nomads Isaac and Jacob wandered with their families and herds all over what is now Syria, Egypt and Israel looking for good pasture land. Like their father, Abraham, they continued to believe in one God. Then a severe shortage of food forced Jacob to settle with his family in the land of Egypt. For a time they were welcome there but a new pharoah made Jacob's descendants, now known as Israelites, his slaves. This slavery was to last for about 400 years.

Key question   Why is Abraham looked upon as the father of the Jewish nation?

> ### Work to do
> In Genesis 12.1–3 God tells Abraham that he has to take his family on a long journey into foreign territory. Read this passage for yourself, looking out for the answers to these questions:
> (a) What is Abraham told that he must leave behind?
> (b) How will Abraham know that he has arrived at the God-given destination?
> (c) What promises does God hold out to Abraham for his future?
> (d) Do you think a Jew might believe these promises have been fulfilled? Give reasons for your answer.

Key words   **Abraham:** the patriarch who left Ur and settled in Canaan in obedience to God's command

BCE: before the Christian Era

Isaac: the son of Abraham and one of the three patriarchs

Jacob: the third of the patriarchs and the son of Isaac

Jewish Bible: the Hebrew text contains 24 books and is divided into the Torah, the Prophets and the Writings

Patriarchs: the title given to three early 'father-figures' of the Israelites – Abraham, Jacob and Isaac

Torah: the most sacred writings in the Jewish faith, recorded in the first five books of the Jewish Bible

1.3 Moses and the Exodus from Egypt

Focusing questions

- What was the Exodus?
- What is the link between the Exodus and the Jewish festival of Pesach?
- What part was played by Moses in leading the Israelites out of slavery and towards their Promised Land?

The Israelites spent about 400 years in Egyptian slavery and this time has left a lasting impression on the Jewish people. So, too, has the escape from that slavery (known as the **Exodus**) and the journey to the promised land of **Canaan**, which took another 40 years. Ever since, Jewish people have relived these events at their spring festival of **Pesach**, or Passover.

Moses

Moses, born in Egypt, during the Israelite slavery, is a key figure in the history of the Jews. The Torah tells us that his mother placed him amongst the reeds on the banks of the Nile when the Pharoah issued an edict ordering the death of all young Hebrew boys. It was there that he was discovered by the Pharoah's daughter, who then brought him up in the royal court as if he were her own son. Later he was forced to leave Egypt in a hurry when he killed an Egyptian soldier who was mistreating a Hebrew slave.

It was whilst Moses was in the desert on his flight from Egypt that God spoke to him out of a burning bush and gave him orders that he was to lead the Israelites out of their slavery and into the Promised Land. At the command of God Moses went to the Pharoah and demanded that he should release the Israelite slaves. The Pharoah refused, so God tormented the Egyptians by bringing ten different plagues on them.

It is the last plague which gives its name to the festival of Passover. The Angel of Death 'passed over' the houses of the Israelites yet struck down the eldest son in every Egyptian household, including that of the Pharoah himself. As a result the Pharoah begged the Israelites to leave Egyptian territory. They began a journey across the wilderness which was to last for 40 years and become the most important event in Jewish history.

Soon, however, the Pharoah changed his mind and pursued the Israelites, finally cornering them on the shores of the Reed Sea (not the Red Sea). According to the Jewish Scriptures it was at this point that God parted the waters of the sea with a strong wind, thus allowing the Israelites to pass through. The waters then came together and swamped the whole Egyptian army.

Across the wilderness

You can follow the journey that the Israelites took once they left Egypt on the map opposite. It was during this journey that Moses spent 40 days and 40 nights on Mount Sinai, where God gave him many laws for the Israelites to follow including **the Ten Sayings** (Commandments), written on stone tablets. God also made a covenant with Moses in which the special nature of his relationship with the Hebrews was established.

Moses himself did not reach the Promised Land. According to the Torah he died on the threshold of the promised land of Canaan. He had done more than enough, however, to ensure his place as one of the most important figures in Jewish history.

Key question **Why is the Exodus of the Jews from Egypt such an important event in Jewish history?**

The Ten Plagues

1. The water of the Nile turned into blood.
2. A plague of frogs covered the land.
3. People and animals were attacked by gnats.
4. Swarms of insects covered Egypt.
5. The Egyptian livestock were attacked by a pestilence from which they all died.
6. Both people and beasts were afflicted by boils.
7. Hail and fire fell on Egypt from heaven.
8. A plague of locusts covered Egypt.
9. Total darkness fell on Egypt for three days.
10. The eldest male child in every Egyptian family was killed.
    (Exodus 7.4–12.30)

During the so-called seder meal, held at the beginning of the Pesach festival, a drop of wine is spilled for each of the Ten Plagues. This is to remind those present that, although the plagues brought freedom for the Israelites, they brought suffering to others.

☐ Can you explain how each plague caused suffering and sadness for those in Egypt who were not Israelites?

Key words **Canaan:** the Promised Land through which the River Jordan flowed and to which the Israelites travelled after leaving Egypt

Exodus: the occasion when Moses led the Israelites out of slavery in Egypt

Pesach: the Jewish festival of Passover

The Ten Sayings: laws given by God to Moses

What was this journey called?

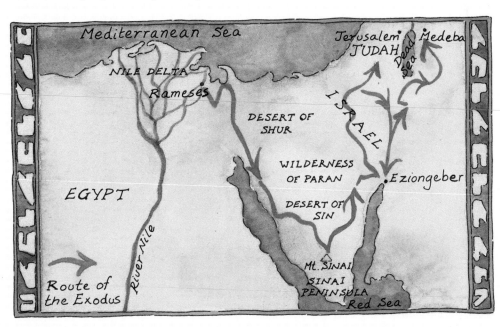

1.4 The Exile

Focusing questions
- Who were the judges?
- Why did the people demand a king, and who was appointed?
- What happened after the death of Solomon?
- What was the Exile?

It took the Israelites a long time to conquer the Promised Land. After they had done so they divided the land amongst the twelve tribes of Israel. Each tribe had its own 'high place' or sanctuary, in which the people worshipped God. Each tribe was ruled over by a 'judge'; two of the best-known judges were Samson and Gideon.

From time to time one tribe or another came under attack from their neighbours, most of whom were easily repulsed. The **Philistines**, however, who occupied the land between the Israelites and the Great Sea, offered a much more serious threat. They had learned how to smelt iron and build chariots and they had hopes of conquering the Israelites and taking their land. The individual tribes could not meet the threat and they asked Samuel, the last of the judges and a prophet, to choose a king for them who could repulse the Philistines.

Saul was the man appointed to carry the hopes of all Israelites.

Israel's kings

However, after two years of continual warfare with the Philistines, Saul was killed in battle. He was succeeded by his son-in-law, David, who became Israel's favourite king, occupying the throne for 40 years. Although he spent most of his time at war with Israel's enemies, including the Philistines, at the time of his death the kingdom was looking reasonably secure. For much of his successor Solomon's reign this prosperity continued, with the king spending seven years building a beautiful temple in Jerusalem.

With Solomon's death, however, the kingdom fell apart. The existence of rival claimants to the throne meant that the tribes in the north set up their own kingdom (Israel) whilst those in the south remained loyal to Solomon's son, setting up a rival kingdom (**Judah**). The kingdoms did not last long. In 721 BCE the powerful nation of Assyria conquered Israel and took the people into captivity. Then, in 586 BCE, the Babylonians took over Judah, destroyed Solomon's Temple and carried off the vast majority of the population into exile. The Jewish people had lost their homeland.

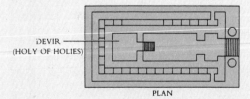

The Temple, built by Solomon. Find out three things about it.

DEVIR (HOLY OF HOLIES)

PLAN

FRONT VIEW

Return from exile

Whilst some of these exiled Jews, and their descendants, returned home in 538 BCE the majority were too comfortable in Babylon and stayed where they were. Gradually they began to filter back to their homeland but, in 63 BCE, their descendants were brought under the heavy hand of the Romans. When the **Zealots** led a revolt in 66 **CE** the Roman response was to destroy the city of

Jerusalem and pull down the Temple begun by Ezra with the first group who returned from exile and enlarged by **Herod the Great**. According to a contemporary account of the event 'not one stone was left standing on another'.

Soon there were many Jewish communities scattered through the Roman Empire and beyond. These people became known as the **Diaspora**. Although reports of occasional revolts in the Holy Land indicate the continued presence of a certain number of Jewish people, the Jewish community was never to return home again in large numbers until the 20th century (see 1.7).

Key question **What happened to Israel between the time of the judges and the taking of the people of Judah into exile?**

A cry from exile

> By the rivers of Babylon,
> There we sat and wept,
> When we remembered Zion.
> Upon the willows in the midst of it
> We hung our harps.
> **(Psalm 137.1,2)**

This psalm was written by someone who had been taken into exile.

☐ Can you find out which city was Zion and why do you think that the remembrance of it caused the exile to weep?

Work to do
Why do you think:
   (a) that each tribe in the Promised Land had its high place for the worship of God?
   (b) that this was called a high place?
   (c) that Israel decided it needed a single leader to deal with the menace of the Philistines?
   (d) that after the death of Solomon the kingdom of Israel fell apart?
   (e) that many exiles preferred to stay in Babylon rather than return to their homeland?

Key words **CE:** Christian Era

Diaspora: the dispersion of the Jewish people outside Israel from the time of the Babylonian exile onwards; the Jewish people living outside the Holy Land after this time

Herod the Great: ruled over the kingdom of Judah from 70 BCE to 4 BCE with great ability but much cruelty

Judah: the southern kingdom of Israel after the division of the country into two parts

Philistines: people who lived along the coast of the Mediterranean Sea and who threatened Israel's existence until David defeated them in battle

Zealots: a fanatical group opposed to the Romans and their occupation of Palestine

1.5 Anti-Semitism

Focusing questions
- What is anti-Semitism?
- What 'crimes' were the Jews accused of committing?
- Which Christian writer incited his followers to attack Jewish property and people?
- What was the 'ultimate crime' committed against the Jews?

Most of the early followers of Jesus of Nazareth were Jews and for some time Christianity remained a movement within Judaism. It was not long, however, before tension began to develop between the old, traditional faith of Judaism and the newly developing Christian religion. Traces of this tension, **anti-Semitism**, can be found in the Christian New Testament and amongst the early Christians. At different times, though, the Jewish people and the Christian Church were both persecuted by the Romans.

Then, in 312 CE, the 'unthinkable' happened and the Roman Emperor, Constantine, was converted to Christianity. This was the catalyst for a new wave of persecution of the Jews to begin. This time, however, the persecution had the support of the Christian Church. There were many Christians who saw this persecution as a suitable punishment for the part that the Jews had played in persuading the Roman governor, Pontius Pilate, to crucify Jesus.

England in the Middle Ages

Augustine, sent by Pope Leo at the end of the 6th century to 'convert' the English to Christianity, arrived to find a Church already well established. It seems that many Roman soldiers and merchants had brought Christianity to England much earlier. Jews, too, began to drift to England although there was not a large influx until William the Conqueror invaded in 1066. These Jews settled in the largest towns. Before long, many had become successful merchants and businessmen and were owed money by a lot of people. Although they tried to be inconspicuous, Christian fanatics singled them out for persecution around the time of the **Crusades** – particularly in such towns as York, Norwich and London. A dreadful massacre, for example, took place in York in 1190 when a Christian mob burnt a large number of Jews to death in a tower. A century later all Jews were expelled from Britain; Jews were not allowed back until 1656.

The charges against the Jews

In the following centuries the Roman Catholic Church held many councils to discuss the Jews and two charges were regularly made against them:

- ☐ that they were responsible for the death of God's son, Jesus Christ;
- ☐ that they murdered Christian children and used their blood for their own religious worship. (This charge, first made in Norwich in 1154, became known as the 'blood libel'.)

Anti-Semitism in Europe

Anti-Semitism was soon widespread in Europe. The great Christian reformer **Martin Luther**, for example, wrote many pamphlets and books attacking the Jews, eventually inciting others to burn down Jewish **synagogues** and to show the Jewish people no mercy at all. This is, of course, just what Adolf Hitler did

14

in the 1930s in Germany. Synagogues were burnt to the ground by Fascists; Jews were arrested and given the most humiliating public work to do. German children were taught in school that the Jewish people were sub-human and should be treated as such. Later Jews were arrested and sent off to be gassed in the many concentration camps. Their only 'crime' was that of being born Jewish.

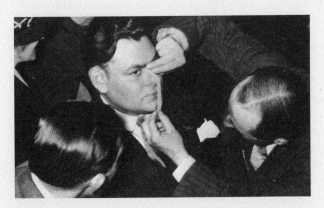

A Jew having his nose measured in Nazi Germany. Why do you think Jews were humiliated in this way?

Key question   What is anti-Semitism and how has it manifested itself?

Work to do

1. Carry out some research into the activities of the Fascists in England just before the Second World War.
   (a) Who was their leader?
   (b) Why were they called the Blackshirts?
   (c) Why did they object to the Jewish presence in England?
   (d) Do you think that such an organisation could exist today? Give reasons for your answer.

2. (a) Apart from Jews can you think of any other group in society which has been, or is, picked upon and persecuted?
   (b) Can you think of *three* reasons why Christians, and others, have picked on the Jews in the past?
   (c) Collect together as many examples as you can to show that anti-Semitism is still alive at home and abroad – use radio, television, newspapers, magazines for your source material.

Key words   **anti-Semitism:** discrimination against, or persecution of, the Jews because of their religious beliefs or race

Crusades: military campaigns by Christian nations in the 11th, 12th and 13th centuries, designed to conquer Palestine and to take Jerusalen from the Muslim Turks to open up the 'holy places' in the Holy Land. Although the main objectives of these armies was to fight the Muslims (whom they called 'infidels') they often attacked Jewish communities and places of worship on the way

Martin Luther: (1483–1546) a German monk who violently opposed the Roman Catholic Church and is widely considered to be the instigator of the Reformation (see 6.5 and 7.1)

Synagogue: a Jewish place of worship

1.6 The Holocaust

Focusing questions

■ What was the Holocaust?
■ How did millions of Jews meet their deaths during the Second World War and where?
■ How have Jews tried to keep the memory of the Holocaust alive?

The facts of the Holocaust speak for themselves. No group of people has suffered as the Jews did during the Second World War (1939–45). Centuries of anti-Semitic hatred and fury exploded in the most frightening example of **genocide** of all time. In just six years 6,000,000 Jews, a million of them children, met their deaths at the hands of the Nazis. They suffered not because they represented any threat to the authorities but simply because they were Jews.

The memorial to the Holocaust at Yad Vashem. Why is it such a suitable one?

The concentration camps

The carnage of the German concentration camps was so horrific that Jewish people speak of those awful years in their history as the **Holocaust**. Between 1935 and 1945 Jews throughout Nazi-occupied Europe were rounded up in vast numbers and shipped off to concentration camps to be gassed. There were 28 such camps in all and their names have become symbols of degradation, inhumanity and death – Dachau, Buchenwald and Belsen among them. One name, however, more than any other has come to symbolise the horror of the gas chambers – **Auschwitz**. At this camp alone 6,000 Jews were being gassed each day by 1944.

Why did the Holocaust happen?

The Nazis claimed that the Jews represented everything that threatened the future of the German nation. Although Jews occupied many positions of importance in the nation, and were very successful in business, they were said to be uncommitted to the future of Germany because their religion appeared to the Nazis to be more important to them than their country. Moreover, the Jews, together with other minority groups such as gypsies and homosexuals, were seen as a threat to the racial 'purity' that Hitler was fanatically trying to achieve in the German people.

Responding to the Holocaust

It was only after the war had finished that the world, and the Jewish community in particular, became aware of the extent of what had happened. Although initially too shocked to make any response at all, the Jewish community soon committed itself to making sure that the world could never forget the Holocaust. Days of memorial were arranged, special prayers were written and places of remembrance established to keep the memory of the Holocaust alive. Several concentration camps were left standing to bear their silent, but powerful witness to the atrocities that had been committed in them. A special memorial to the Holocaust was built at Yad Vashem, in Jerusalem. The name itself means 'a place and a name' – the place is a bare room lit by a single candle and the names are those of the different concentration camps written on the floor. Also at Yad Vashem there is a line of trees, 'the Avenue of the Righteous', with a tree planted for every Gentile who helped a Jew during the war.

Key question   **What was the Holocaust, and why were the Jews singled out for such inhuman treatment?**

Inscription at Dachau

Dachau, in southern Germany, housed one of the worst of the concentration camps. It is now a museum and this inscription is to be found on one of its walls:

PLUS JAMAIS

NEVER AGAIN

NIE WIEDER

NIKOGDA BOLSHE

☐ Can you recognise each of these languages? Why do you think that the notice was written in these languages?

☐ Apart from Jews, can you think of any other minority groups in society which could be singled out for persecution by an unscrupulous government? What makes them so vulnerable?

☐ Can you think of *three* ways in which the rest of the world could make sure that nothing like the Holocaust ever happens again?

Work to do

In the Middle Ages Jews were told, 'You cannot live amongst us as Jews'; in the modern age Jews were told, 'You cannot live amongst us'; in the Nazi era Jews were told, 'You cannot live.'

(a) Carry out some research of your own into *one* other occasion, apart from the Holocaust, when the Jews were singled out and persecuted.

(b) Why do you think that this particular group of people has been persecuted far more than any other?

Key words   **Auschwitz:** Polish extermination camp which opened in 1940 and was soon receiving people from all over Europe at a rate of at least one train-load (at least 7,000 people) a day

genocide: attempt to exterminate a race, nation, etc.

Holocaust: literally 'immolation by fire, total destruction'

1.7 Reaching the Promised Land

Focusing questions
- What is Zionism?
- What declaration helped the Jews to return to their homeland?
- When and how was the State of Israel established?

After the Jews rebelled against the Romans in 66 CE they were scattered all over the known world. As a result of this dispersal (the Diaspora) only a handful of Jews remained in their homeland. During the following 1800 years most of the people who moved into Israel were Arabs. By 1900, in fact, only one person in ten living in Israel was a Jew.

Zionism

Scattered as they were throughout the world, Jews rarely found a home. They were looked upon as outsiders and persecuted as such. Usually their lives were hard. Yet, despite hardship, the vast majority of them kept their religious traditions and language intact. Above everything else they retained a deep-seated hope that one day they would be able to return to their homeland. An important step towards achieving this goal was taken in 1897 when an Austrian Jew, **Theodor Herzl**, set up the **Zionist** movement. One supporter asked the question that thousands of others were asking: 'Why should we be aliens (outsiders) in foreign countries when the land of our forefathers is still able to receive us?'

The first step in the return to 'the land of our forefathers' was taken when Jews began to settle in Palestine. The second came in 1917, when the British foreign secretary, Arthur Balfour, wrote to the president of the English Zionist Federation, Lord Rothschild, encouraging the Zionists to send greater numbers of settlers. This letter became known as the Balfour Declaration. By 1936 Zionist immigrants made up more than 30 per cent of the region's population, a fact which greatly alarmed the indigenous Arabs, some of whom reacted by taking violent action against the settlers. The British, who had occupied Palestine since the end of the First World War, gave military support to the Jews and by the start of the Second World War Arab resistance had been defeated.

The State of Israel

At the end of the war there was an urgent need to resettle the thousands of Jews who had survived the Holocaust (see 1.6) but many of those who set sail for Palestine found their boats turned away by British forces. As a consequence, Zionist resistance fighters began a campaign of violence against the occupying army, which was still under attack from Arab forces opposed to any admission of Jewish immigrants at all.

In an attempt to resolve the problem, a meeting of the United Nations agreed on a proposal to divide Palestine equally between the two parties, with just over half the land going to the Jews. This was unacceptable to the Arabs. When British forces withdrew in 1948, the Zionists, led by David Ben-Gurion, immediately declared the establishment of the independent State of Israel. The homeland promised by their prophets thousands of years previously was at last in the hands of the Jews. The Palestinians on the other hand mostly fled the country, and remain without a homeland to this day.

Yet the new country was far from secure. In 1948 and 1949 a bloody war

The British were trying to stop these Jews entering Palestine. Why?

with Israel's Arab neighbours left over 1,000,000 Palestinian Arabs homeless. Many of them are still refugees forty years later. Even today, after two wars, in 1967 and 1973, the Arabs and the Israelis have still not been able to reach a peace agreement.

Key question **How was the ancient promise to restore the Jews to their homeland fulfilled?**

The Balfour Declaration on Palestine

His Majesty's Government view with favour the establishment in Palestine of a national home for the Jewish people, and will use their best endeavour to facilitate the achievement of this object, it being clearly understood that nothing shall be done which may prejudice the civil and religious rights of existing non-Jewish communities in Palestine, or the rights and political status enjoyed by Jews in any other country.

☐ What did the British government promise the Jewish people in this declaration?

☐ What did it promise those people who were not Jews but who lived in Palestine?

Work to do
Read these extracts:

☐ *Also I will restore the captivity of My people Israel,*
And they will rebuild the ruined cities and live in them
. . . And they will not again be rooted out from their land
Which I have given them. (Amos 9.14,15)

☐ *Thus says the Lord, I will return to Zion and will dwell in the midst of Jerusalem. Then Jerusalem will be called the City of Truth . . . Behold, I am going to save My people from the land of the east and from the land of the west; and I will bring them back, and they will live in the midst of Jerusalem, and they will be My people and I will be their God, in truth and righteousness. (Zechariah 8.3–8)*
(a) What were the Jewish people to do on their return to their homeland?
(b) What name was to be given to Jerusalem on God's return?
(c) What future promises do both Amos and Zechariah hold out to the Jewish people?

Key words **Theodor Herzl:** (1860–1904) Austrian founder of the Zionist movement who envisaged both a home for Jews in Palestine and a political Jewish state

Zionist: term describing the movement which aimed at founding a Jewish state in Palestine

1.8 Groups within Judaism

Focusing questions

- **What is an Orthodox Jew?**
- **What is Chasidism?**
- **What is neo-Orthodoxy?**
- **What is a Reform Jew?**

As we noticed in 1.1, Jewish identity is strengthened by a sense of shared history and a feeling of common destiny as God's chosen people. Yet not all Jews think, or worship, alike. They can in fact be divided into two main groups – **Orthodox** and **non-Orthodox Jews**.

Orthodox Jews

Orthodox Jews are in the majority in all Jewish communities except those in the USA. These believers insist that the old traditions of the faith must be kept alive and honoured. Since they hold the Torah to be the actual word of God, as written down by Moses, its laws must be obeyed. This is because these laws are a reflection of the will of God and, as such, are timeless and eternal.

Orthodox Judaism is broken down into other smaller groupings. One particularly important grouping is the **Chasidim**, who insist that an even stricter code of belief and behaviour must be followed. The Chasidim stand out from other Jews in their refusal to wear Western clothes. They insist on wearing the clothes that their ancestors wore in the ghettos of Eastern Europe in the 17th

Which Jews are very strict about dress?

century when the movement was first formed. Some Chasidic believers in the USA do not wear ties since they insist that these separate the heart from the head when both should combine in the service of God. However, a cord is worn around the waist to divide the higher from the lower part of the body. They also grow locks of hair over their ears. Their worship emphasises joy and spontaneity and this makes it very different from more Orthodox Jewish worship.

During the 19th century, in Germany, Rabbi Sampson Raphael Hirsch developed an approach to Judaism which combined what he saw as the best features in Chasidism with the best of Orthodoxy. He believed that Jews should take on what was best in the Western way of life, such as clothes and a modern language of communication, and combine it with living a full Jewish life in obedience to God. His approach became known as **neo-Orthodoxy**.

Non-Orthodox Jews

Since the end of the 18th century there have been Jews who have sought to 'modernise' Judaism and to make Jews more acceptable in a non-Jewish society. Such Jews have been variously called Progressive, Reform and Liberal Jews. Although there are some small differences between them they all emphasise that true religion is constantly developing and that old ways of worshipping may not be suited to the modern world. Non-Orthodox Jews also allow women to play a much more central role in their religious worship. Some non-Orthodox communities are led by a woman rabbi.

Key question **What are the main differences between Orthodox and non-Orthodox Jews?**

Work to do

1. **Invite an Orthodox and non-Orthodox Jew to speak to your class and to answer your questions. Make a list of your own questions but include the following if you like:**
   (a) What is your attitude to the Torah?
   (b) How do you worship in your synagogue?
   (c) Do you follow strict rules about food and clothing and, if so, what are they? Why do you consider such laws to be important or unimportant?
   (d) What is your attitude towards Jews who think differently to you?

2. **After their visit imagine that you have a pen-friend abroad who is interested in finding out more about the Jewish faith. Write a letter to him or her explaining some of the differences which exist between Orthodox and non-Orthodox Jews.**

Key words **Chasidim:** ultra-conservative Orthodox Jews

neo-Orthodoxy: a variety of Judaism which attempts to combine a traditional Jewish approach with the best of the surrounding culture and way of life

non-Orthodox Jews: Jews who believe that the Torah is a human document and that not all of it is relevant to life today

Orthodox Jews: Jews who believe that the Torah is the most important part of the Hebrew Scriptures and that all of its laws must be kept

2. WHAT DO JEWS BELIEVE?

2.1 What do Jews believe about God?

Focusing questions

- ■ Why do Jews assume that God exists?
- ■ What do Jews believe about God?
- ■ What is the Covenant that was made between God and the Israelites and what obligations does it place on both parties?

The very first verse of the Jewish Scriptures assumes that God exists:

In the beginning God created the heavens and the earth
(Genesis 1.1)

and requires no proof of that existence. God simply is, and two facts of life are taken to underline this: the existence of the universe that God has created; the existence and the history of the Jews as God's chosen people.

The Jewish God

Each morning and evening Jewish people recite the **Shema**. This prayer is taken from the Jewish Scriptures and declares the most basic Jewish belief about God – that there is only one God. Furthermore this God has no rivals and there is no limit to His power – He has created all of the forces of nature and they are under His control. In addition all human activity is controlled by God and accepting this brings a sense of unity to the whole of life.

Yet, as exalted and all-powerful as this God is, He is not remote from the world that He has made. Jews speak of God as being 'shekinah', that is present everywhere, and according to the **Talmud** 'There is no place without the Shekinah.' God can be seen and experienced in the whole of nature in all its infinite variety. God controls the whole of this universe and yet stands over and beyond it.

The Covenant

The Jewish Scriptures start by painting a picture of God creating the natural order and the human race. Then a particular family, Abraham's, is 'chosen' by God. The Scriptures speak of God entering into an agreement, called the **Covenant**, with the descendants of this family. There were two sides to this agreement as there are to every covenant:

- ☐ The nation of Israel must remember God at all times, serve Him and keep all of His laws.
- ☐ God will remain faithful to the nation of Israel, will continue to be that nation's God and will treat its members as His own special people.

The commandments (mitzvot)

As we saw in 1.3 the Jewish Scriptures tell us how Moses led the Children of Israel out of Egyptian slavery towards the Promised Land. During that journey they arrived at the foot of Mount Horeb (or Mount Sinai), where, in the mountain, Moses received the commandments or law (mitzvot) that God wanted Israel to keep. There are 613 such commandments in all – 248 of them are positive commandments ('Thou shalt . . .') and 365 are negative mitzvot ('Thou shalt not . . .'). The Ten Sayings or Commandments are part of these mitzvot.

Key question **What is distinctive about the Jewish belief in God?**

The Shema

Hear, O Israel ! The Lord is our God, the Lord is one ! And
you shall love the Lord your God with all your heart and with all
your soul and with all your might.

(Deuteronomy 6.4,5)

☐ Can you find out why this prayer is called the 'Shema'?
☐ How is the worshipper expected to react to the 'oneness' of God?

Children learning
the Shema.

Work to do
A traditional story is told about Rabbi Joshua ben Hananiah, who lived in the 1st century CE. He was challenged by a powerful potentate of the time:

'I want to see your God,' the Emperor said to the rabbi.
'You cannot,' replied the rabbi.
'But I insist,' repeated the Emperor.
The rabbi's response was to point up to the blinding light of the noonday sun.
'Look into the sun,' he said.
'I cannot,' answered the Emperor.
'If you cannot look at the sun, which is one of the servants who stands in the presence of the Holy One, praised be He,' said the rabbi,' then is it not even more evident that you cannot see God?'

What was the rabbi trying to teach the Emperor about God?

Key words **Covenant:** a binding agreement made between God and the people of Israel

Shema: the Jewish prayer which states the belief that there is only one God

Talmud: a huge collection of discussions about practical and moral questions collected between the 1st and the 6th centuries CE (see 2.3)

23

2.2 What do Jews believe about the Messiah?

Focusing questions

- What is meant by the word 'Messiah'?
- On which occasions, in particular, have Jews looked forward to the coming of a Messiah?
- Do all Jews look forward to the coming of one person or is there another way of understanding the Messiah?

There have been many occasions in Jewish history when the people have either been persecuted or taken into exile. On these occasions, in particular, they have looked forward to the coming of the **Messiah**, God's Anointed One, who would arrive on earth at the end of time. Possessing infinite righteousness, wisdom and powers of leadership, this person would defeat all of Israel's enemies and usher in God's kingdom of peace and prosperity on earth. In that kingdom, as one of Israel's prophets tells us, 'the wolf will lie down with the lamb.'

The promise of the Messiah

For hundreds of years Jews have lived with this promise of the coming of the Messiah who would follow in the footsteps of the great Jewish king, David. In the Bible many of the Psalms describe what kind of person this Messiah was expected to be:

- ☐ He will be called God's son.
- ☐ He will bring with Him the blessings that God intends for His people on earth.
- ☐ He will establish God's kingdom on earth, which will be based on the principles of law and justice.
- ☐ He will rout and destroy all of Israel's enemies.
- ☐ He will rule over the whole world forever.

The same theme was taken up by the prophets beginning with Isaiah in the 8th century BCE. These prophets tended to look forward to the birth of a human rather than a divine figure. Isaiah describes the picture that he has in his mind of the Messiah in this way:

> *For a child will be born to us, a son will be given to us . . .*
> **(Isaiah 9.6)**

Jews have always been discouraged by their rabbis from trying to work out, or guess, just when the Messiah will appear. Although many people have claimed to be the Messiah many Orthodox Jews are still waiting for God's Anointed One to appear. On the other hand there are many Reform Jews who have questioned this traditional understanding of the Messiah. Instead they are looking forward to the time when all people, working together, will establish God's kingdom of love, peace and righteousness on earth.

Leading up to the kingdom

Whether the Messiah is a single human being or the whole of humanity, Jews agree that before God's purposes on earth can be truly fulfilled various events must take place:

☐ the return, to their Promised Land, of Jews scattered over the whole earth;
☐ the abolition of all injustice, war, discrimination and immorality;
☐ a world society based on the principles of truth and justice;
☐ a religion in which all people everywhere will share, based upon the Jewish experience of one God.

Key question **What do Jews believe the Messiah will be like when he comes to deliver Israel from her enemies?**

The prophets talk about the Messiah

For a child will be born to us, a son will be given to us;
And the government will rest on His shoulders;
And His Name will be called Wonderful Counsellor,
  Mighty God,
Eternal Father, Prince of Peace.
There will be no end to the increase of His government
  or of peace . . .
(Isaiah 9.6,7)

Behold, the days are coming,' declares the Lord,
'When I shall raise up for David a righteous Branch;
And He will reign as king and act wisely
And do justice and righteousness in the land.'
(Jeremiah 23.5)

☐ How many different statements can you find in these two extracts about the Messiah and the kind of kingdom he will establish? Make a list of them.

Work to do

1. Read this paragraph carefully and copy it into your book filling in the missing blanks.

On the many occasions in their history when Jews have been persecuted or taken into exile they have longed for a _____who would deliver them from their enemies. Such a figure would follow in the footsteps of the great Jewish figure, _____. In the _____, a book in the Jewish Bible, the _____ was someone who would be called _____ _____, would defeat all of Israel's _____and establish God's _____on earth. Amongst those prophets in the Jewish Bible who looked forward to the coming of the _____were _____and _____.

2. Why do you think that the idea of a Messiah continues to be attractive to Jews even though their people have been waiting for him for centuries?

Key words   **Messiah:** title meaning 'anointed one', used in the Jewish Scriptures to refer to kings and the High Priest. Later it came to refer to a future leader who would come to deliver the Jews from their enemies.

2.3 What do Jews believe about their holy books?

Focusing questions
- Which three parts go to make up the TeNaKh?
- What is the Pentateuch?
- What is the Talmud?

The Bible

The most important document for all Jews is their Bible. Written in Hebrew this document (the TeNaKh) is made up of three parts, the Torah, the Prophets and the Writings.

The Torah (the teaching) is the part of the TeNaKh which Jews prize most highly. It covers the first five books of the Jewish Bible – Genesis, Exodus, Leviticus, Deuteronomy and Numbers. (These five books are also known as the **Pentateuch**.) In its opening chapters the Pentateuch deals with the creation of the world. The narrative soon moves on through the stories of the patriarchs to an account of Moses leading the Israelites out of slavery to the borders of their Promised Land.

An important part of Jewish worship is the reading aloud of set portions from the Torah. Indeed the whole Torah is divided up into 54 sections since this is the maximum number of shabatot (plural of '**shabat**') that there can be in a single year. Public readings in the synagogue are then given from the **Sefer Torah** on sabbath mornings and afternoons, festival mornings and on Monday and Thursday mornings. It is considered a great honour to be chosen to read from the Torah. The person reading follows the passage in Hebrew by using a **yad**, or silver pointer.

This rabbi is using a yad to mark his place in the Torah. The small photo shows it in more detail.

The Prophets (Neviim) were considered to be the spokesmen of God and their writings are amongst the most beautiful in the Hebrew Bible. Public readings from the Prophets also take place to 'accompany' those being given from the Torah.

The Writings (the Ketuvim) are considered to be of lesser value than the Torah and the Prophets, but the Writings do contain the Psalms, which are used regularly in synagogue worship. Readings from the Writings do take place – usually on festival days.

The Talmud

For centuries an enormous number of judgements, opinions and practices governed the way that the Jews were expected to act. These important pieces of information were kept alive by word of mouth and passed down from generation to generation. Then, in about 200 CE, they were collected together in a document called the 'Mishnah'.

Scholars then began to discuss the Mishnah and to add even more material of their own. The new material was collected together to form the 'Gemara'. Together the Mishnah and the Gemara form the Talmud. This enormously large volume has had a tremendous effect upon the way that Jews have lived their lives for centuries.

Key question   Which books make up the Hebrew Scriptures? How are they read in the synagogue?

> ### Work to do
>
> **1. Several mistakes have been made in this paragraph. Find out the mistakes and copy a corrected version of the paragraph into your book.**
>
> Jewish people have the greatest possible respect for their Bible (TiNaKh), which is made up of three parts. The first five books of the Bible (the Neviim) are the books of the Law or the Torah. Passages from this are read regularly in the synagogue when a special scroll, called a yad, is used. Readings from the Writings (the Torah) usually accompany those from the Prophets. The Torah is a collection of judgements and opinions which has had a considerable effect on the Jewish community since it was first compiled around 400 BCE.
>
> **2. Can you find out:**
> **(a) who is responsible for writing, and producing, the Sefer Torah and how the great reverence which Jewish people have for their Bible is continued in this process?**
> **(b) at which Jewish festival the old yearly cycle of reading the Torah ends and the new one begins?**
> **(c) what importance Jews today attach to the Torah?**
> **(d) who is eligible to read from the Sefer Torah in the synagogue and why it is considered to be a great honour to do so?**

Key words   **Pentateuch:** (also known as the Torah) the first five books of the Hebrew Bible – Genesis, Exodus, Leviticus, Deuteronomy and Numbers

Sefer Torah: the actual scroll from which the Torah reading is taken

shabat: the Hebrew word for sabbath day

yad: a silver pointer, in the shape of a hand, which a person uses to make sure that he doesn't lose his place whilst he is reading the Torah

2.4 What do Jews believe about life after death?

Focusing questions
■ What do the Principles of Moses Maimonides have to say about life after death?
■ What is the link in Judaism between the Messianic Age and the age to come?
■ What do Jews believe about heaven and hell?

Although there is no formal creed of Jewish belief the best-known attempt to draw one up was made by Moses Maimonides in the 12th century. His 'Thirteen Principles of Faith' are included in the **Siddur**. Two of these principles deal with the afterlife:

☐ God will reward the righteous and punish sinners both in this world and the next.
☐ There will be a resurrection of the dead.

The afterlife

There is very little mention in the Jewish Scriptures about the afterlife. It seems that Jews were encouraged to live God-fearing lives on earth and to leave the question of what happened after death to God. Certainly, the belief expressed by Moses Maimonides that:

☐ God rewards the righteous in a life to come;
☐ God punishes the wicked;
☐ God will bring all people back to life.

developed long after the Scriptures were completed. For centuries Jews took seriously the warning in the Talmud against any unhealthy speculation about what might happen in the world to come since 'no eye has seen it'.

The coming Messianic Age

Over the centuries Jewish minds have been much more concerned with the coming of the Messianic Age on earth than they have been with any speculation about life after death (see 2.2). The Messiah's work will be to make this world a better place by establishing God's kingdom here. There is, however, a hint that this Messianic kingdom is but a step on the way to a world to come. This world to come is the end to which God is said to be finally working. It is also the end to which every Jew aspires – to find a place in God's eternal kingdom.

Between earth and heaven

Although the details are very vague the Jewish Scriptures do suggest that a time is coming, during the reign of the Messiah on earth, when all of the righteous Jews will be brought back from the dead. When this happens life will reach its perfect form – the kingdom of God here on earth.

Yet this kingdom, no matter how long it lasts, will not endure for ever: at the end of the world the non-Jewish dead will be brought back to life and judged by God and his angels. Of these non-Jews the unrighteous will be judged and sent to hell (gehinnom). Unlike the form that hell takes in other religions, however, in the Jewish faith it is not a place of everlasting torment. According to Jewish tradition it lasts for a maximum of twelve months, during which time the souls are cleansed from their sins so that they are eventually suitable to enter into the presence of God. Meanwhile the righteous non-Jews are immediately transformed so that they can share in the world to come.

In the past Jews have spoken about such topics as heaven, hell, Satan, angels and the resurrection of the body but these topics are only a matter of limited interest nowadays. Their recent history has been so much taken up with pain and suffering that it seems pointless to speculate about the afterlife. They are content to leave the details of that in the hands of God.

Key question **What is the Jewish idea of life after death?**

A Jewish midrash

A Jewish midrash is a teaching or commentary from a Jewish rabbi. One such midrash says:

People in this world fulfil commandments and do not know the value of what they have gained. In the world to come they will realise what they have achieved.

☐ What, according to this quotation, is the difference between this life and the world to come?

Work to do

1. (a) Write down a list of *seven* things that most Jewish people believe about life after death.
   (b) Jews seem to be very vague about the precise details of life after death. Muslims and Christians say a lot more. Do you think it is better to be imprecise about such a topic or do people appreciate knowing as much about it as possible?

2. The following comment was made by Mrs Jacobs, an elderly Jew, in a series of programmes, 'Worlds of Faith', broadcast in 1983:
   When I was about 13, I was at one of the many schools I attended in my childhood, and it was one of the happiest schools I attended. And I can remember in a discussion . . . my teacher saying, 'Heaven isn't a place, it's a state of mind.' This is one of the very few things I remember so clearly from my school days and it's something I think about from time to time; and when we say when someone has died, may her soul rest in peace, I think it means that that person should be spoken of and thought of and remembered by the people who were close to them while they were here in this life.
   (a) What do you think this Jewish woman understood by the phrase 'Heaven isn't a place, it's a state of mind'?
   (b) How does Mrs Jacobs understand 'life after death'?

Key words **Siddur:** the Jewish daily prayer book (as distinct from the prayer book which is used for festivals)

3. THROUGH THE JEWISH YEAR

3.1 Shabat (the sabbath day)

Focusing questions

■ Which two 'events' are commemorated on each sabbath day?
■ How does the sabbath day begin?
■ What happens during the service held on the morning of shabat?
■ How does the sabbath day draw to a close?

Origin of the sabbath day

In the Jewish community the sabbath day, or shabat, is a very important day. The custom of resting from all work on this day (the word 'sabbath' actually means 'ceasing') is an ancient one and marked out the Israelites as being different from those around them who expected slaves and servants to work seven days a week.

In the Jewish Scriptures the sabbath day is linked with two biblical events and these are recalled each time the day is celebrated.

God made the heaven and earth in six days and rested on the seventh to enjoy the fruit of his labour. On the principle that what is good for God must be good for those He created, Jews are expected to rest on the seventh day of each week to refresh themselves for the week ahead.

The story of the rescuing of the Israelites from Egyptian slavery should be a reminder to all Jews that the destiny of their nation is firmly in God's hands. It is important to recall this divine deliverance, therefore, every sabbath day.

At home on the sabbath day

The sabbath day starts traditionally at sunset on Friday evening and finishes at nightfall on Saturday. The more orthodox Jews consult a special Jewish calendar for the area in which they live to find out the exact time that the sun sets. All of the food is prepared before the day begins and the table is laid for a special sabbath meal. Then, at sunset, the woman of the house lights two candles to welcome in the sabbath day. As she does so she says a blessing. The whole family then gathers for a ceremony called **Kiddush**, which involves:

☐ the blessing and drinking of wine (the symbol of joy);
☐ the blessing of the day itself;
☐ the blessing by the father of his wife and children.

The shabat meal begins with the breaking of bread. There are always two loaves (**hallot**) on the sabbath table and these are twisted or plaited in a distinctive way. Songs are sung and the meal ends with a prayer of thanksgiving.

The Talmud details 39 different kinds of work which have to 'cease' as soon as the sabbath begins and these cover more or less everything that involves physical effort – no matter how small. So Jewish people who keep the sabbath day faithfully do not go to work or school; do not carry out any housework or homework; do not use public transport; do not prepare or cook food and do not go shopping. Instead they look upon the sabbath day as a God-given opportunity to worship, study and enjoy a time of recreation with their family.

Celebrating the sabbath

An important part of the sabbath day is the service held in the synagogue on

Saturday morning. As people arrive they wish each other 'Shabat shalom' (a peaceful sabbath). During the service which follows, the Torah is ceremoniously taken from the **ark** to be read aloud.

Then, at the end of the day, there is another ceremony. At **Havdalah** wine is drunk, a special candle with several wicks is lit and a spice-box is opened to wish everyone a sweet week. The parting greeting is 'shavua tov' (a good week), as the wine is poured over the candle to extinguish it.

Key question   **Why do you think the sabbath day has been described as 'the jewel in Israel's crown'?**

The sabbath day

> *For in six days the Lord made the heavens and the earth, the sea and all that is in them, and rested on the seventh day; therefore the Lord blessed the sabbath day and made it holy.*
> **(Exodus 20, 11)**

> *the sabbath day is a sabbath of the Lord your God . . . and you shall remember that you were a slave in the land of Egypt . . .*
> **(Order of service for the sabbath day)**

The shabat meal.

The prayer of blessing

> *Blessed are you, O Lord our God, ruler of the universe who makes us holy*
> *through doing his commandments and has commanded us to light the Shabat candles.*
> **(Order of service for the sabbath day)**

☐ What should be remembered on the sabbath day?
☐ Why did the Lord God bless the sabbath day?
☐ What does the photo tell you about the shabat meal?

Key words   **ark:** the cabinet in the synagogue in which the scrolls of the Torah are kept

hallot: loaves specially baked for eating on the sabbath day

Havdalah: the service in a Jewish house at the end of the sabbath day

Kiddush: the special prayer recited at the beginning of the sabbath day and on other holy days

3.2 Rosh Hashanah and Yom Kippur

Focusing questions
- What is the shofar and what part does it play in Rosh Hashanah and Yom Kippur?
- What is the theme of Rosh Hashanah?
- Whose example do Jews follow on Yom Kippur?

The Jewish New Year, **Rosh Hashanah**, is one of the most solemn days in the Jewish calendar. It is celebrated in the autumn (September–October) and ushers in ten days of heart-searching and repentance. Many Jews celebrate Rosh Hashanah over two days.

A Day of Judgement

The main symbol associated with Rosh Hashanah is the **shofar** or ram's horn. This instrument is capable of producing three different sounds and these are used to call the people to repent:

- a long, drawn-out sound which calls on everyone to listen;
- a broken, plaintive sound which represents the repentant people of Israel;
- a sharp, staccato sound which is reminiscent of the sobbing of repentance.

On Rosh Hashanah the shofar is blown 100 times. Just as trumpets announce the presence of a human king so the shofar pronounces the coronation of God. It is also calling the people:

- to look back to the creation of the world when God made all things perfect;
- to look forward to the time of judgement when God will call all people to account for the way that they have lived.

This theme of judgement is uppermost at Rosh Hashanah and in the days that follow. The rabbis of old taught their congregations that on Rosh Hashanah three books are opened in heaven in which the deeds of all people are inscribed. The books are then sealed. One day everyone will be called to account for what is sealed in the books.

The New Year also looks forward to the coming time when the Messiah (see 2.2) will redeem the Jews and the whole human race.

Yom Kippur

In Jewish tradition **Yom Kippur** is ranked as the holiest day of the year. Beginning after sunset on the ninth day of Rosh Hashanah it is marked by 25 hours of prayer and fasting following the example of God's angels who do not, according to tradition, eat or drink, but spend their time praising God. So, on this one day, Jews attempt to serve God as if they were angels. They follow the teaching of the Talmud which forbids eating, drinking, washing, sexual intercourse, anointing with oil, and wearing sandals or leather shoes, on Yom Kippur.

According to tradition, Satan is able to tempt the Jewish people every day of the year except on Yom Kippur. On that day God declares to Satan: 'You have no power over them today; nevertheless go and see what they are doing.' Satan finds all Jews fasting and dressed like angels in white clothing. He returns to God embarrassed. He says: 'They are like angels and I have no power over them.' At this God binds Satan in chains and declares to His people: 'I have forgiven you all.'

To Jewish people, then, Yom Kippur is, above all else, a day of forgiveness (the Day of Atonement). As they seek forgiveness from all relations, friends and neighbours that they have wronged, so God extends His forgiveness to them.

Key question **How do the festivals of Yom Kippur and Rosh Hashanah bring Jews to reflect on the way in which they behave throughout the year?**

The shofar calls Jewish people to look forward to the time of judgement. What sounds does it make and what are their significance?

The three books

On Rosh Hashanah, three books are opened in the heavenly court: one for the wicked, one for the righteous, and one for those in between. The fate of the righteous is inscribed and sealed there and then: Life. The fate of the wicked is inscribed and sealed then and there: Death. The fate of those in between remains undecided from Rosh Hashanah to Yom Kippur. If during those days, their deeds show their worthiness, they are inscribed and sealed for Life; if not, they are inscribed and sealed for Death.

(Jewish legend)

☐ What is the fate of the righteous and the wicked on Rosh Hashanah?
☐ How long do the others have to determine their fate?

> ### Work to do
> **Read the story of the near sacrifice of Isaac in Genesis 22. This account is read in the synagogue on Rosh Hashanah.**
> **(a) Why do you think that the blowing of the shofar reminds worshippers of Abraham's willingness to sacrifice his own son?**
> **(b) Why do you think the story of Abraham and Isaac is read on Rosh Hashanah?**

Key words **Rosh Hashanah:** the Jewish New Year, which marks the beginning of ten days of repentance for the Jewish nation

shofar: the ram's horn which is blown many times during Rosh Hashanah and once at the end of Yom Kippur

Yom Kippur: the most solemn day in the Jewish calendar, which brings to a close the days of penitence begun at Rosh Hashanah

3.3 Sukkot and Simhat Torah

Focusing questions

- Why are tabernacles built in the home and in the synagogue during Sukkot?
- What are the 'four species' and what part do they play during the festival?
- Why is Simhat Torah an important festival in the Jewish calendar?

In ancient Israel there were three 'pilgrimage' festivals which drew all scattered Jews, wherever they were living, to the Temple in Jerusalem. The autumn harvest festival of **Sukkot** was one of these pilgrimages and it celebrated the years that the Israelites had spent wandering in the wilderness after leaving Egypt. This completed the story told at the other two pilgrimage festivals – the Passover (see 1.3), at which the journey out of Egyptian slavery was relived, and **Shavuot**, which looked back to the giving of the law to Moses on Mount Sinai. Jews still celebrate these three festivals today.

Living in shelters
Sukkot begins five days after Yom Kippur (see 3.2) and continues for seven days. Many families build their own tabernacle or booth and spend some time living in it during the festival. Other families 'camp out' in a tabernacle built in the local synagogue. This is a reminder of the temporary shelters (sukkot, singular sukkah) that housed the Israelites during their wanderings in the desert. The sukkot also act as a reminder that life is fragile and that no one stays long on their journey through it. We are all dependent on God for every step of that journey. This dependency is symbolised by the fact that everyone who sits in a sukkah should be able to see through the roof – and so be open to God.

The four species
The harvest theme of the festival is emphasised by the four symbols most closely associated with it (the four species). The use of these is laid down in Leviticus 23.40:

- ☐ the 'fruit of the goodly tree' which is taken to be the 'etrog' and looks rather like a lemon;
- ☐ a palm branch which is known as a 'lulav';
- ☐ a bough of a leafy tree, twigs of myrtle called 'hadas';
- ☐ a willow branch which is known as 'aravah'.

On several occasions, during synagogue services, the lulav is taken up in the right hand and the etrog in the left. They are waved, for example, during the recital of the Hallel psalms (Psalms 113–18).

Simhat Torah
The celebration of **Simhat Torah** follows immediately after the ending of Sukkot. It is on this day that the annual cycle of readings from the Torah ends and a new cycle begins, without a break. By reading the last chapter of Deuteronomy and the first chapter of Genesis the people are symbolising the eternal continuity of the Torah.

During the service the scrolls of the Torah are carried around the synagogue, and sometimes into the streets, to the accompaniment of great rejoicing and happiness. Children kiss the scrolls, carry banners and receive sweets. In most Jewish communities this is the happiest day of the year.

Key question **What is the significance to the Jewish community of the festivals of Sukkot and Simhat Torah?**

The feast of the Booths

On the fifteenth of this seventh month is the Feast of Booths for seven days to the Lord. On the first day is a holy convocation [meeting]; you shall do no laborious work . . . on the eighth day you shall hold a holy convocation . . . it is an assembly. You shall do no laborious work.
    (Leviticus 23.34–36)

☐ What is another name for the festival of Sukkot?
☐ How long is this festival to last?
☐ What must people not do during this festival?

A family celebrating Sukkot. What does the shelter commemorate?

> ### Work to do
> The festival of Sukkot commemorates events from the past history of the Jewish nation.
> (a) Explain the agricultural link of this festival.
> (b) What is the historical event recalled during this festival?
> (c) Some Jewish festivals are extremely solemn whilst others are very happy occasions. Can you find out which category Sukkot falls into, and why?

Key words **Shavuot:** the Jewish festival of Weeks, which is celebrated fifty days after Passover (see 3.7)

Simhat Torah: the day on which the old cycle of reading the Torah ends and the new cycle begins

Sukkot: the Jewish festival held at the end of the harvest in October and lasting for seven days

3.4 Hanukkah (the festival of Lights)

Focusing questions

- What event is remembered at Hanukkah?
- How do Jews today celebrate Hanukkah?
- What traditions are celebrated at Hanukkah and how do they fit in with the theme of the festival?

The festival of **Hanukkah** ('dedication') is celebrated for eight days in December. It is different from the other Jewish festivals in that it is not mentioned in the Bible. The festival is based upon the recapture and rededication of the Temple in Jerusalem in 165 BCE. This building, so important to the Jews, had been taken and dedicated by the Greeks to their god, **Zeus**.

The origin of Hanukkah

After the recapture of the Temple by a Jewish army, led by Judas the Maccabee, an eight-day celebration was held. During this time the Temple was cleansed and purified. Every pagan object taken into the holy building by the Greeks was removed. The **menorah** (candelabrum) was found to be badly damaged so a temporary menorah was made out of the spears of the warriors. In this way the weapons of war were transformed into agents of peace.

The Jews could then find only enough oil to keep the Everlasting Light burning before the Holy Ark for a single day. As this light symbolised the continuous presence of God with His people, it was never allowed to go out. Miraculously, on this occasion, the supply lasted for eight days until a new supply could be prepared. It is this miracle that is celebrated at Hanukkah.

The Everlasting Light.

Celebrating Hanukkah today

Lights and rejoicing are the two key elements in the celebration of Hanukkah. On each night of the festival a candle is lit in a menorah, so that by the end of the festival eight candles have been lit. The first of these candles, the 'servant' candle, is called a shamash and is used to light the rest. The candles must be lit early in the evening, soon after sunset, so that even the youngest member of the family can enjoy the excitement of the festival. As each candle is lit this prayer is offered:

These lights are holy and we are not permitted to make use of them, but only to see them in order to thank Your name for the wonders, the victories and the marvellous deeds.

Traditionally at Hanukkah Jewish children play with 'dreydels'. These are spinning tops which have a different Hebrew letter on each of their four sides. The letters are the initial letters of four Hebrew words which mean 'a great miracle took place there', referring, of course, to the miraculous supply of oil.

Hanukkah is very much a family festival and the people eat food cooked in oil, like doughnuts, to remind them of the single jar of oil in the Temple. They also enjoy a traditional Jewish 'chip', or potato pancake (also cooked in oil), known as a 'latkes' (levivot). Presents are always given and received – sometimes on each of the eight days of Hanukkah. No wonder that Hanukkah is a very popular festival with Jewish children!

Key question   **Why is Hannukah different from other Jewish festivals and what miracle forms the basis of the celebrations?**

The birth of Hannukah

And they built the sanctuary and the interior of the Temple and consecrated the courts. And they made new holy dishes and they brought the lampstand and the altar of incense and the table into the Temple. And they burned incense on the altar, and lighted the lamps on the lampstand, and they lighted the Temple . . . Then Judas and his brothers and all the congregation of Israel decreed that the days of the rededication of the altar should be observed at their season, every year, for eight days, beginning with the twenty-fifth of the month of Chislev, with gladness and joy.
(I Maccabees 4.48–59)

☐ Why is the festival of Hanukkah also called 'the festival of Lights'?
☐ How long should the celebration of this festival last for and when should it start?

Work to do
Explain the link between each of the objects shown opposite and the festival of Hanukkah.

Key words   **Hanukkah:** the Jewish festival of Lights, which falls each December

menorah: kind of candelabrum, first used in Jewish worship in the old Temple

Zeus: the chief of the Greek gods, who dwelt on Mount Olympus

3.5 Purim (the festival of Lots)

Focusing questions
■ What is unusual about the story of Esther?
■ What happened to Haman?
■ What happens in the synagogue when the story of Esther is read at Purim?

The festival of **Purim** takes place in late winter. It commemorates the spectacular events recorded in the biblical book of **Esther**. In this book, set in ancient Persia, the Jews were saved from destruction through the God-inspired actions of Esther.

The story behind the festival

There are four main characters in the story:

☐ the Persian king, Ahasuerus;
☐ the commander-in-chief of the king, Haman;
☐ the Jewish queen, Esther;
☐ Esther's Jewish uncle, Mordecai.

Haman wanted to destroy all of the Jews living in Persia and he persuaded the king to allow him to do so. They were only defeated by the wisdom of Mordecai and the courage of Esther. In the end Haman was hanged on the very gallows that he had built for others. Because Haman cast 'lots' to determine the appropriate day for the Jewish massacre this festival is known as Purim, which is the Hebrew word meaning 'lots'.

God is not mentioned at all in the biblical account of the story of Esther. He is, however, believed to be behind the scenes controlling what is going on. Indeed it is this aspect, the hidden hand of God, which gives Purim its power and importance by showing that in the end good will always triumph over evil.

Celebrating Purim

On this day, in the synagogue, the whole story of Esther is read from a special handwritten parchment scroll. In modern Israel it is also broadcast on radio and television. During the reading in the synagogue pandemonium breaks out every time the name of Haman is mentioned. All of the children in the congregation try to drown the name out by using rattles, cap pistols, alarm clocks or by writing the name on the soles of their shoes and stamping their feet!

In addition, on Purim, worshippers:

☐ give gifts to the poor;
☐ send food parcels to other families;
☐ eat a festive meal at which wine is expected to flow freely.

Jewish tradition is opposed to drunkenness but in the story of Purim the king killed his first wife because he was drunk and if this had never happened Esther would not have become queen and the Jewish nation would have been wiped out. The Talmud states that on Purim a person should drink until they cannot distinguish between 'cursed is Haman' and 'blessed is Mordecai'. This is the only time of the year, then, when Jews are encouraged to get drunk.

Key question What part did God play in defeating Haman and safeguarding the Jewish nation at the time of Mordecai and Esther?

The Purim meal.
What are the children
doing?

A Purim prayer

We thank you for the wonders, for the heroic acts, for the victories, for the marvellous and consoling deeds which you performed for our fathers in those days at this season. In the days of Mordecai and Esther, in Shushan the capital, when the wicked Haman rose up against them, he sought to destroy, kill and exterminate all Jews, both young and old, little children and women, on one day, and plunder their possessions . . . then you, in your great mercy, upset his plan and overthrew his design, and made his acts recoil upon his own head. And you performed a wonder and a marvel for them, therefore we thank your great name.

☐ What do the people thank God for at the festival of Purim?
☐ What did Haman try to do?
☐ Who upset Haman's plan?
☐ What happened to Haman?

Work to do

You may need to carry out some research of your own before answering these questions.

(a) How had Esther, a Jewess, come to be the queen of a Persian province and why were the lives of the Jewish people threatened?

(b) How did the festival of Purim get its name?

(c) Describe one theme which comes out of the story of Esther and is kept alive in the celebration of Purim today.

(d) What is the spiritual significance of the festival of Purim?

Key words **Esther:** the heroine of a book of the Bible which is named after her

Purim: (festival of Lots) Jewish festival which, according to tradition, is the only festival which will be continued in the world to come

3.6 Pesach (the festival of Passover)

Focusing questions
■ What event is commemorated at Pesach?
■ What is the seder meal?
■ What is the significance of the different items on the table for the seder meal?

There is no more popular Jewish festival than Pesach or Passover. Originally a spring festival, Pesach has for centuries been celebrated to remember the Exodus, or deliverance, of the Israelites from Egyptian slavery (see 1.3). Although this event took place some 4,000 years ago, for Jews it still remains the most important demonstration of God's power. They are expected to relive the event at Pesach as if they were really there.

The seder meal

Although there are services in the synagogue during Pesach, the festival revolves very much around the home. Before it begins the house is thoroughly cleaned from top to bottom to remove all traces of leavened bread. This search is a game in most Jewish houses but it does make a very important point. When the Jews left Egypt they needed to pack so quickly that they did not have time to take any yeast with them. This meant they could only eat flat loaves (matzot) during their 40 years in the wilderness. For the duration of Pesach, therefore, only unleavened bread is eaten.

On the eve of Passover, which lasts for two days altogether, the men go to the synagogue and then return home for a special meal, the **seder** meal. This starts with the blessing of wine – four glasses of wine are drunk during the meal as a reminder of God's four promises to Moses. There are a number of symbolic items on the table in front of the family to help them to 're-create' the Exodus experience. Two of these items are not eaten:

☐ a roasted shank-bone representing the lamb which was slaughtered each year in the Temple, until its destruction in 70 CE;
☐ a roasted egg which recalls the Passover sacrifice in the Temple. The Jews have not practised sacrifices of any kind since the Temple was destroyed.

These two items recall religious practices which have long since ceased. The other items on the table, however, are tasted to act as reminders of the Exodus:

☐ three matzot loaves of unleavened bread;
☐ maror or bitter herbs, which recall the bitterness of slavery in Egypt;
☐ a green vegetable, usually parsley, which is dipped into salt water to remind everyone of the tears of the Hebrew slaves in captivity;
☐ haroset – a mixture of nuts, wine and apples – which symbolises the cement the Jews were forced to make to build homes for their Egyptian masters.

A fifth cup of wine also stands on the table although no one drinks it. This cup shows that God's redemption will come at some time in the future when, according to Jewish tradition, the coming of the prophet Elijah will foreshadow the coming of the Messiah.

Key question Why is the Passover such an important Jewish festival and why is it such a clear demonstration of God's power?

The four promises

Say therefore to the people of Israel, 'I am the Lord and I will bring you out from under their bondage, and I will redeem you with an outstretched arm and with great acts of judgment, I will take you for my people, and I will be your God . . .

(Seder service on Passover night)

☐ What are the four promises that God made to Israel?

The seder table.

Work to do

1. Read these words from the Haggadah:
In every generation everyone should regard himself as if he personally had come out of Egypt.
How does the celebration of the Passover help a Jewish person to relive the events of the Exodus?

2. Look carefully at the photograph of the seder table.
(a) Name three foods that you can see on the plate.
(b) What is the spiritual significance of the foods you have named in (a)?

3. Why do you think that Jewish people go to such great lengths to re-create the events of the Exodus when they celebrate Pesach?

Key words   **Haggadah:** special book telling story of Exodus from Egypt, and God's delivery of the Jews from slavery

seder: the word means 'order' in Hebrew, and refers to the special order of service in the meal that takes place on the eve of Passover – this order is recorded in the Haggadah

41

3.7 Shavuot (the festival of Weeks)

Focusing questions
- **What are the two elements of the celebration of Shavuot?**
- **What was every Jewish farmer expected to present to God at Shavuot?**
- **How is Shavuot celebrated today?**

Although it was originally a festival to celebrate the summer harvest, Shavuot (see 3.3) was soon linked to one of the most important events in Jewish history – the occasion when Moses received the Torah (teaching) from God on Mount Sinai. Jews look upon the Torah as God's greatest gift to them.

Shavuot – a harvest festival

During the original harvest festival all farmers brought their first fruits to the Temple, where they offered them as a sign of their thankfulness to God. As they did so they said:

> *My ancestor was a stranger when he went down to Egypt but there he became a great and strong nation. Then the Egyptians afflicted and enslaved us. So God brought us up out of Egypt with a mighty hand and glorious miracles into a land flowing with milk and honey. And now, behold, I have brought the first of the fruit of the land which God has given me.*

This agricultural link stays with Shavuot today: the synagogue is beautifully decorated with fresh fruit, plants and flowers for the festival.

The giving of the law

Today, however, the link of Shavuot with the giving of the Torah is much more important than its connection with the harvest. This is because it was at Mount Sinai that a weary group of ex-slaves was transformed into a nation with an identity of its own. The whole foundation of that nation was to be the laws that Moses received. There were over 600 of them in all, but the most important, by far, were the Ten Sayings or Commandments.

Celebrating Shavuot

Traditionally Jews stay up on the night of Shavuot reading the Torah. To keep themselves awake they drink coffee and eat dairy produce, especially cheesecake. Honeycake is also a traditional Shavuot food – reminding the people that the Torah is sweet to the spiritual taste.

Apart from the reading of the Ten Sayings all Jews also read the book of **Ruth** on Shavuot. This beautiful love-story from the Jewish Scriptures tells how Ruth was converted to the Jewish faith after helping with the gleaning at harvest time. This makes it, of course, a very appropriate reading for this particular festival.

Shavuot is also known as the 'festival of first fruits'. In Israel today many farmers bring baskets of bikkurim (ripe first fruits) to a central area. They are expressing their joy and pride in the fruitfulness of the land that God gave to His people centuries ago.

Key question What are the two main themes of the festival of Shavuot?

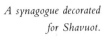

A synagogue decorated for Shavuot.

The Ten Sayings

I am the Lord your God who brought you out of slavery from the
land of Egypt.
You shall have no other gods before me.
You shall not make any graven image.
You shall not take the name of the Lord your God in vain.
You shall remember and keep the Sabbath Day holy.
Honour your father and mother.
You shall not kill.
You shall not commit adultery.
You shall not steal.
You shall not bear false witness against your neighbour.
You shall not covet your neighbour's wife, nor anything that
belongs to your neighbour.
(Exodus 20.1–17, translated in the Jewish Prayer Book)

☐ How many of these sayings deal with a man's relationship with God and how many with his relationship with his neighbour?

☐ In these sayings one very good reason is given for loving God. What is it?

Work to do

1. Look at the photograph above.
(a) Which important agricultural event was originally celebrated at Shavuot?
(b) Which event in Jewish history does the festival now commemorate?
(c) Explain, in your own words, how Jewish worshippers combine the original agricultural background with the later historical meaning in their celebration of Shavuot.

2. *You shall also count for yourselves from the day after the sabbath 'the end of Passover', from the day when you brought in the sheaf of the wave offering; there shall be seven complete sabbaths. You shall count fifty days to the day after the seventh sabbath; then you shall present a new grain offering to the Lord.* (Leviticus 23.15–16)

☐ **According to this quotation how many days must elapse between the festival of Passover and Shavuot?**

Key words   **Ruth:** a Gentile who was married to a Jew. After he died leaving her childless she remained loyal to her mother-in-law, Naomi, before remarrying another Jew, Boaz

43

4. JEWISH WORSHIP

4.1 The synagogue

Focusing questions

- Why were synagogues built in the first place?
- What is the ark and why is it such an important feature in a synagogue?
- Apart from worship, how is a synagogue used?

We are not sure when synagogues first came into being, but it seems likely that when the ancient Jews were exiled to Babylon (see 1.4) they started to form synagogues because they could not attend the Temple in Jerusalem. They simply gathered together wherever they were to pray and to praise God. Even when the Temple was later rebuilt the Jews continued to build synagogues which were used not only for worship but also as courts of law and as schools.

The worship that went on in these early synagogues was less formal than that in the Temple and was led by a chazzan, or reader, since no priests were available. After the Temple was destroyed by the Romans in 70 CE it was never rebuilt. This was because Jewish tradition taught that God alone could rebuild the Temple. Although Jews still continue to pray for the Temple to be rebuilt no one expects it to happen. Jewish worship has for centuries been centred around the home and the synagogue.

Inside a synagogue

Although some religious ceremonies are performed in the home, many Orthodox synagogues do have public services twice a day. In addition, of course, Jewish people come together on the morning of shabat and on special feast days.

Inside a synagogue the central feature is the ark (see 3.1), which is set into the wall whose outside faces Jerusalem. Since the congregation always faces the ark during services it too faces the holy city. The Sifrei Torah (see 2.3) are stored in

The ark. What is kept in it?

the ark, but sometimes during the service they are removed to be carried in procession around the synagogue.

The **Ner Tamid** (the Everlasting Light – see 3.4) burns above the ark and a nine-branched candlestick stands in front of it. In many synagogues two tablets of stone are found above the ark. On these are inscribed an abbreviated from of the Ten Sayings or Commandments. The **Star of David** is commonly found in synagogues.

In the centre of most Orthodox synagogues in Britain is a **bimah** (raised platform), although it may, in some synagogues, be placed in front of the ark. It is to the bimah that, during a service, the Sefer Torah is taken to be read. As the bimah is a raised platform, the reader of the scroll must 'go up' to the Torah. This act symbolises the belief that God's word, the Torah, is higher than man.

In the old Temple not only were men and women separated but also Jews and Gentiles, who were excluded from the main building. Each group had its own 'court'. In most Orthodox synagogues there is still a gallery for women, while men sit on the ground floor. Reform Jews, however, allow males and females to sit together.

The synagogue as a community centre

Apart from being places of worship synagogues are also used as community centres. Wedding receptions and bar mitzvah celebrations are invariably held in the synagogue, which also hosts other meetings and lectures. In addition most synagogues offer youth clubs, crèche facilities and gatherings for old people.

Key question   What are the main features of a synagogue?

Work to do

1. A modern guide to a synagogue says:
   Visitors are often surprised at the apparent lack of formality in synagogue services . . . people may be seen talking to one another, entering and leaving the synagogue and children play among the worshippers . . . there are certain parts of the service when, provided the individual worshipper is not disturbed, his neighbours will talk to one another.
   (a) Invite a local rabbi or practising Jew into your class so that you can find out more about synagogue worship and try to discover whether this description is an accurate picture of a synagogue service *or*
   (b) Visit a local synagogue on the sabbath so that you can share in the service.

2. Make a list of all the symbolic features that you would find in a synagogue and the meaning of their symbolism.

Key words   **bimah:** desk, or platform, in a synagogue from which the Torah is read

Ner Tamid: Everlasting Light, originating in the old Temple and symbolising the presence of God with His people

Star of David: star shape made of two interlocking triangles. Although older examples have been found in Jewish cemeteries and synagogues, it has only been used as a distinctively Jewish symbol since about the 12th century

4.2 Prayer

Focusing questions

■ How often each day is a Jew expected to pray?
■ What are the symbols used by a Jewish man whilst he is praying?
■ What is the Amidah?
■ What is the Shema and why is it an important prayer?

Although a Jew is expected to be constantly aware of God's presence, there are three times in the day when prayer is most important: in the morning; at noon; in the evening.

In addition, there are prayers to be said at mealtimes, on holy days, to the Torah and on special months in the year. Nearly all of these prayers are formal written texts in which the same words are repeated every time. One of the most important Jewish prayers is the **Amidah**.

Symbols of prayer

A unique feature of Jewish prayer is that it is usually accompanied by several external symbols. According to Jewish tradition, prayers offered together by a congregation are far more meaningful than those said by a person on his or her own since it is the congregation that upholds and sustains the individual.

The three visible symbols of prayer are:

The tallit (prayer-shawl): in the Orthodox Jewish community the **tallit**, a shawl which has fringes on each corner, is only worn by male worshippers on the eve of the Day of Atonement (Yom Kippur). In Reform synagogues, however, it is worn by women as well.

The tefillin (leather boxes) are worn by men and are strapped to the arm (close to the heart) and to the forehead (close to the mind). The **tefillin** are not worn on shabat or during festival days.

The yarmulka (skull-cap): most Orthodox male Jews wear a **yarmulka** at all times, not only during prayer. In Reform synagogues, however, most worshippers do not cover their heads.

Another important Jewish symbol is the **mezuzah**, which is a small container with passages from the Jewish Scriptures inside. This is fixed to the doorposts of Jewish houses and offices to symbolise God's presence among those inside. It reminds people as they go in and come out that they are guided by God's presence and love.

The Shema

As we have already seen (2.1) the Shema is the most important Jewish prayer, or declaration of faith, since it reminds all Jews of those beliefs which are to be found at the very centre of their faith:

☐ that God is one;
☐ that human beings are expected to love God;
☐ that all Jews are under an obligation to learn and teach;
☐ that all Jews are expected to pursue a holy life.

A copy of the Shema is placed inside each tefillin and mezuzah, and Jews repeat the Shema each morning and evening. The order of prayer stipulates that two benedictions are to be said before the Shema and that the Amidah should follow. Each order of daily prayer ends with the Alenu (meaning 'upon us is the duty'), which confirms the worshipper's belief in the sovereignty of God and the expectation that God will usher in the Messianic Age.

Key question   **Which symbols does a Jewish man use when he is praying and what do they symbolise?**

> *O Lord, our God, hear our cry!*
> *Have compassion on us and pity us;*
> *Accept our prayer with loving favour . . .*
> *For You mercifully heed Your people's supplication.*
> *Praised are You, O Lord, who is attentive to prayer.*
> **(The Amidah)**

☐ In this prayer the worshipper asks God for four things. What are they?

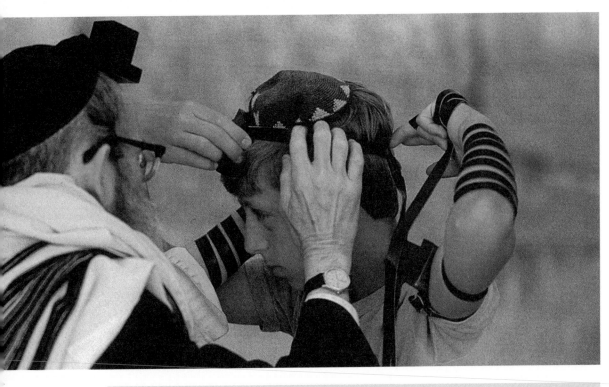

A Jewish man dressed for prayer.

Work to do
Look at the photograph. This man is wearing three symbols of his faith. What are they?

Key words   **Amidah:** a series of 19 benedictions which form the central core of Jewish worship

mezuzah: small container holding biblical texts inscribed on parchment

tallit: fringed Jewish prayer-shawl of white material striped with black and blue

tefillin: small, leather boxes containing selections from the Jewish Scriptures

yarmulka: skull-cap worn by Orthodox Jews

47

4.3 Leaders within the community

Focusing questions
- What is the cantor responsible for in the synagogue?
- What task, formerly carried out by a child's father, is now performed by a mohel?
- What tasks are performed by a rabbi?

The Jewish religion does not have priests as such. Instead it relies on a wide variety of people to meet the needs of the Jewish community inside and outside the synagogue. The most important of these are:

The cantor (chazzan)

In larger synagogues a cantor is employed to lead the congregation in their singing. This is important since the playing of musical instruments on the sabbath day is classified as 'work' and so they play no part in worship. The cantor's main responsibility is to chant parts of the prayers on shabat and other festivals. He also takes part in weddings and funeral services.

A scribe from the Yemen. Why is he a leader in his community?

The scribe

To scribes falls the important task within the Jewish community of copying out the new Torah scrolls and the small parchments which are placed in the tefillin and mezuzah (see 4.2).

The mohel

Traditionally a child's father was given the delicate task of circumcising his eight-day-old son. In almost all Jewish communities now, that task is carried out by a professional mohel (circumciser) as you will find out in 5.1.

The shochet

The shochet is a Jew specially trained to slaughter animals according to the laws laid down in the Jewish Scriptures. Only the animals that have been killed

48

properly by a shochet are **kosher** and considered fit for a Jew to eat. The laws by which animals are to be killed are called **Shechita**.

The rabbi

In the Jewish religion a rabbi is not an 'intermediary' between God and the worshipper. Each man or woman is responsible in the sight of God for their own salvation. The rabbi is someone who is highly trained and educated in all aspects of the Jewish faith and is expected to play several roles:

☐ to take part in sabbath worship, lead the prayers, read from the Torah and deliver his/her sermon to the people;

☐ to conduct weddings and funerals, and to comfort the bereaved;

☐ to educate members of the congregation in the traditions and beliefs of the Jewish community;

☐ to visit members of the community who are sick or unable to attend the synagogue – a rabbi may also act as a Jewish chaplain to the local hospital, college or prison;

☐ to form, with two other rabbis, a **bet din** – often this 'court' decides on matters which Jewish people prefer to have dealt with in a religious court rather than in a court of law;

☐ to act as an ambassador for the Jewish religion in the community.

Key question **Which particular responsibilities are spread through the Jewish community and who carries them?**

Work to do

1. Try to invite one of the people who play an important part in the Jewish community into your school. Find out just what they are expected to do and why they consider their work to be important.

2. What do you think that this quotation from the Talmud means: 'One should not live in a town that has no scribe.'

Key words **bet din:** a 'house of judgement', a Jewish court which decides on disputes between Jewish people

cantor: the song-leader who leads much of the public sabbath worship in a synagogue

kosher: literally 'fit' – a word to describe any food that is killed or prepared according to laws laid down in the Jewish Scriptures

mohel: a professional who carries out circumcisions on young Jewish boys

rabbi: literally a 'teacher' – a Jewish minister who teaches the religion and often leads the worship as well

scribe: someone who copies out, and repairs, the scrolls of the Torah

Shechita: traditional laws concerning the way animals are killed

shochet: man in the Jewish community who is authorised to kill animals according to the Shechita

5. THE MILESTONES IN LIFE

5.1 Birth and circumcision

Focusing questions
- What is circumcision?
- Why was circumcision originally carried out when the baby was eight days old and what is the custom today?
- What is the significance of circumcision within the Jewish community?

According to an old Jewish **midrash** 'the whole world rejoices when a child is born' and this sums up the Jewish attitude to the birth of a new baby. Every new life is a gift from God and so must receive an open welcome into the family. If the baby is a boy then he will undergo **circumcision** on the eighth day after birth – a custom that has remained unchanged since the time of Abraham.

Brit millah (circumcision)

According to the Book of Genesis the decision to circumcise all Hebrew males was first taken after a conversation between God and Abraham. This makes circumcision the oldest Jewish religious custom of all. Abraham was told that this circumcision was a sign of the Covenant (or agreement) between God and the Jewish people.

Just as Abraham was responsible for circumcising all of the males, young and old, in his household, so Jewish tradition has always held the father responsible for circumcising his own children. The operation, however, is rather delicate and so special circumcisers (called 'mohalim') are trained to carry it out.

This circumcision takes place in the baby's home and since tradition does not allow the baby's mother to be present, he is carried into the gathering by his grandmother. The baby is then handed over to the sandek (godfather), who passes him on to his father. The father places the baby in a chair, Elijah's chair, since this Jewish prophet is believed to be invisibly present throughout the ceremony. The sandek then holds the child on his knees whilst the mohel carries out the circumcision. The foreskin of the baby's penis is removed by a stroke of a sharp knife and the skin is then secured to prevent further growth. As he does this the mohel recites a blessing over the child before the child's father pronounces a further blessing:

> *Praised be Thou, O Lord our God, ruling spirit of the universe,*
> *who has commanded us to enter into the covenant of our father Abraham.*

The people present respond by saying:

> *As he entered into the covenant, so may he enter into the love of*
> *the Torah, into the marriage canopy and into the life of good deeds.*

The baby receives his name and a drop of wine is placed on his lips. The father then drinks the remainder of the glass. A family celebration completes what everyone (except, perhaps, the baby) looks upon as a very happy occasion.

What does circumcision mean?

A baby becomes a Jew because he has a Jewish mother and not because he is circumcised. His circumcision does have two important implications, however:

☐ The baby receives his father's blessing and, since the time of Abraham, this has always been very important.
☐ The baby becomes 'religiously' clean and is welcomed into membership of God's Chosen Race. The 'sign' in his flesh will constantly remind him of this.

Key question   **What is the spiritual significance of circumcision for Jewish people?**

God and circumcision

> *God said further to Abraham . . . every male among you shall be circumcised. And you shall be circumcised in the flesh of your foreskin; and it shall be the sign of the covenant between Me and you.*
> **(Genesis 17.9–11)**

☐ How would circumcision act as a permanent reminder of the agreement made between God and the Jewish people?

Work to do

1. An old rabbi is reported as saying this about circumcision: *Know that a man is not called by the name of man except through ritual circumcision. Without it he is called an evil spirit and not a man . . .*
(a) What do you think that he meant?
(b) Why do you think that he placed such a high degree of importance on circumcision?

2. Explain the meaning of this blessing said over the baby by the mohel: *Praised be thou, O Lord our God, king of the universe, who has sanctified us with your commandments and given to us the rite of circumcision.*

Key words   **circumcision:** the religious act of cutting off the foreskin of a baby boy's penis

midrash: commentary – the Midrash is a large and very important commentary on part of the Jewish Scriptures

5.2 Bar mitzvah

Focusing questions
- What is the meaning of bar mitzvah?
- What are the important elements in the bar mitzvah ceremony?
- Which 'events' take place at a bar mitzvah?

Every Jewish boy begins his religious education at a very early age. One reason for this is to introduce him to the **mitzvot** (commandments) which outline what his duties and responsibilities will be when he becomes an adult. A Jewish boy is considered by his community to have reached adulthood on his 13th birthday. The occasion is marked by him becoming a **bar mitzvah** (son of the commandment).

The ceremony

Becoming a bar mitzvah is a very important milestone in the life of every Jewish boy. In the ceremony which is held to commemorate the event, usually on the first shabat after his 13th birthday, several important events take place:

- The boy is called forward for the first time to read, in Hebrew, from the Sefer Torah. Since this privilege is only extended to adult males in the Orthodox community, it is a public announcement that the boy has come of age. As he reads he follows the words with the silver finger pointer.
- The boy receives his father's blessing. The father thanks God that he has now been freed from any responsibility for the boy's sins and rejoices that his son is now old enough to carry this responsibility for himself.
- The parents arrange a meal (the seudah) eaten after the ceremony to show the value of the commandments that he has taken on. During this meal the boy delivers his derasha (mini-sermon) in which he thanks everyone for their gifts, thanks his parents for all that they have done for him and expresses his own religious hopes for the future.

What makes bar mitzvah so important?

There are three main reasons why this milestone is so important for every Jewish male:

- The boy who has come of age, the bar mitzvah, is given the full privileges and responsibilities of an adult male Jew. He is also able to wear the tallit and tefillin (see 4.2) on the appropriate occasions.
- At any time in the future he can be called up in the synagogue to read the whole, or part, of the Torah reading for that day. All Jewish men consider this to be a great privilege.
- In many synagogues the ceremony is looked upon as an opportunity for a person to renew his Jewish commitment. It is assumed that he would not pass through it unless he was serious about his dedication to the work of God and the Jewish community.

Key question What is the significance to a Jewish boy of becoming a bar mitzvah?

Concerning the upbringing of a Jewish child the Talmud declares:

When a child begins to speak his father should speak with him in the holy tongue and teach him Torah. If he does not do so it is as if he buries him.

☐ What should a Jewish father do as soon as his son starts to speak?

☐ What do you think the 'holy tongue' is?

☐ What must a father teach his son?

☐ What do you think the Talmud means when it says: 'If he does not do so it is as if he buries him'?

Work to do

1. These are the words that the father prays as he blesses his son during the bar mitzvah ceremony:

Blessed is the One who has freed me from responsibility for the boy's sins.

What do you think he means?

A boy being blessed as he becomes bar mitzvah.

2. As we shall see in 5.3 some synagogues (Reform synagogues) hold a similar ceremony (bat mitzvah) for girls, who are deemed to reach adulthood at the age of 12.

(a) Do you think some kind of recognition that a person has passed out of childhood into adulthood is a good thing?

(b) What do you think of the view that girls are ready to take on adult responsibilities at 12 and boys at 13?

(c) At what age do you think most young people are ready to assume adult responsibilities?

3. Invite a Jewish person who has gone through bar mitzvah or bat mitzvah to talk with your class about the experience. Remember to find out not only what happened but also what the service meant to them, personally.

Key words **bar mitzvah:** literally 'son of the commandment', ceremony held in the synagogue for 13-year-old boys to mark their attainment of adulthood. The term is also used as an adjective and applied to boys who have been through this ceremony

mitzvot: literally means 'commandments' – a term which has come to include all of the duties and responsibilities required by God of the Jews

5.3 Bat mitzvah

Focusing questions

- **What was the Jewish confirmation service?**
- **What is bat mitzvah?**
- **What is bat hayil and how does it differ from a bar mitzvah?**

No ceremony exists in Orthodox Judaism to celebrate the time when a Jewish girl comes of age on her 12th birthday. The reason for this is that, unlike a boy, a girl does not take on any new religious responsibilities when she becomes an adult. Such a ceremony, however, is an important part of religious worship in Reform synagogues.

Confirmation

During the early 19th century many German, French and Italian Progressive synagogues replaced the tradition of bar mitzvah with a confirmation service. This new service had several distinctive and important features:

- [ ] Prior to the service boys and girls were taught the Jewish faith together rather than separately, as was the case in the more traditional synagogues.
- [ ] Boys and girls were confirmed together.
- [ ] The confirmation ceremony took place at a later age than bar mitzvah – usually when the young person was around the age of 16.
- [ ] Whilst the ceremony could be held at any time during the year, it came to be associated with Shavuot and was held as part of the celebrations for that festival.

A Jewish girl reads from the Torah. What kind of synagogue would allow this?

For some years this confirmation service was popular in the USA and western Europe but now there has been a general return to the traditional bar mitzvah.

A ceremony for girls

To recognise the importance of women in the Jewish community Reform synagogues have recently developed a ceremony for girls to parallel the bar mitzvah. This is intended to encourage women to play a much more active role in Jewish worship instead of the largely passive part that they play in Orthodox worship. So, at the age of twelve, girls become **bat mitzvah** (daughters of the commandment) in a ceremony which varies from synagogue to synagogue. It is held on the shabat, carried out on a number of girls at the same time, and involves the girls reading from the Torah, just as the boys do.

Bat hayil

In recent years some Orthodox synagogues have introduced the status of bat hayil (daughter of valour). In this ceremony the girl does not read from the Torah, which remains a male privilege, but she does read other passages taken from the Prophets or the Writings.

Key question   What is bat mitzvah?

Work to do

1. Make a list of three ways in which a bat mitzvah ceremony is different from the bar mitzvah services.

2. Read these two statements carefully. The first is written by a Jewish girl and the second by a non-Jewish boy.

    (a) *I look back to the time when I became bat mitzvah with real pride. To me it not only underlined the fact that I was a member of the Jewish nation but also that I had passed from being a child into being an adult. Somehow, from that time onwards, I began to think of myself as being an adult and I was not afraid to take on some extra responsibilities.*

    (b) *I think that it is very strange that there is no ceremony to mark the time when most children become adults. After all, it is such an important time in a person's life and you'd think they'd do something to make it special, wouldn't you? I have a Jewish friend who often speaks to me about her bat mitzvah.*

    ☐ Do you agree with these young people that the transition from being a child to being an adult is too important for it to be allowed to slip past almost unnoticed?

    ☐ Do you think that something like a bar mitzvah for everyone would be a good idea?

3. Read Proverbs 31.10–31 and then explain why a girl reaching adulthood in an Orthodox synagogue is said to be bat hayil.

Key words   **bat mitzvah:** ceremony held in Reform synagogues at which 12-year-old Jewish girls are recognised as bat mitzvah, or daughters of the commandment

5.4 Into marriage

- What is the chuppah?
- What is the difference between erusin and chuppah?
- What is distinctive about a Jewish wedding?

The Jewish community has always recognised the importance of marriage. The rabbis taught the people that it was within the plan of God for everyone and this is recognised in the circumcision ceremony when the hope is expressed that the baby will enter into the **chuppah** (marriage canopy).

A Jewish wedding

On the shabat before the wedding the groom is called forward in the synagogue to read from the Torah or the Prophets. When he has finished he is greeted with cries of 'Mazel tov' – Good luck. Then, in the hours preceding the wedding, it is traditional for the bride and groom to fast. This allows them to seek God's forgiveness for all their past mistakes and provides them with the opportunity to start their married life together with a clean slate.

Before the wedding can take place the **ketubah** must be prepared and signed in the presence of two male witnesses. This is a formal marriage contract which specifies what will happen to the bride if her husband divorces her, or dies before she does.

Traditionally there are two parts to the wedding ceremony:

- The erusin (betrothal) is the pre-marriage commitment that binds a man and a woman together without allowing them to live together.
- The chuppah, or canopy, symbolises the reception of the bride by the groom into his home.

In a modern Jewish wedding, however, these two aspects are brought together. For the ceremony itself the groom stands under the chuppah facing Jerusalem, with the rabbi and cantor opposite him. The bride is brought to join him by her mother and mother-in-law to be. Then the following ritual takes place:

- The cantor sings a greeting to the couple asking for God's blessing on them.
- The first of two glasses of wine is poured out, symbolising the couple's common destiny.
- The groom takes a plain gold ring and declares to his bride: 'Behold you are sanctified 'made holy' to me with this ring, according to the law of Moses and Israel.' In accepting the ring the bride shows that she is freely entering into the marriage.
- The ketubah is read aloud before being handed to the bride. The cantor then chants the seven benedictions of wedlock which end with the words: 'Blessed are you, O Lord, who gladdens the bridegroom with the bride.'
- The bridegroom then breaks a wine glass beneath his feet to shouts of 'Mazel tov' from the guests. This is a traditional Jewish way of lamenting the destruction of the Temple in Jerusalem centuries ago.

Key question How does the Jewish wedding service underline the importance of the married life that the couple are about to begin together?

The chuppah. What does this word mean?

Taking a new wife

> *When a man takes a new wife, he shall not go out with the army, nor be charged with any duty; he shall be free at home one year. and shall give happiness to his wife whom he has taken.*
> **(Deuteronomy 24.5)**

☐ Why do you think that the husband in Israelite society was given a year free of duty to spend with his wife?

Work to do

1. A traditional Jewish story underlines the belief that, although marriage is very important, it can also be very difficult. A rabbi was asked by a middle-aged Roman woman, who was not a Jew, what the God that Jews believed in had been doing since He created the universe. 'Making marriages,' he said to her, 'that is as difficult as dividing the waters of the Red Sea.' To prove the rabbi wrong the woman took a thousand of her male slaves and a thousand of her female slaves and 'married' them to each other. By the morning they were all miserable. The woman was forced to admit that it was not easy to make a happy marriage.

☐ What is the main point of this story and how is this point underlined by the marriage service?

2. During the wedding service, as he gives his ring to his bride, the groom says:

> *Behold you are sanctified to me with this ring, according to the law of Moses and Israel.*

What do you think that he means by these words?

Key words   **chuppah:** literally 'canopy' – the word has now come to mean the whole marriage ceremony. Modern writers refer to the canopy under which the couple stand as a symbol of God's presence

ketubah: the marriage document received by a Jewish bride setting out the duties of the bridegroom towards her

5.5 Death

Focusing questions

- What is the chevra kadisha and what role does it play in death in a Jewish community?
- What is the Kaddish prayer?
- What are the stages of mourning through which the bereaved person moves?

All Jews hope that they will be granted the strength to pray the last prayer (see the words of the last prayer opposite) before they die. In the last hours of a person's life a rabbi does not have to be present since it is the responsibility of the **chevra kadisha** to perform the last acts of kindness and make the burial arrangements.

After death

Once a person has died, the sequence of events is as follows:

☐ The eyes and mouth of the corpse are closed by a near relative. The body is then washed and wrapped in a single white linen shroud. In the case of a man it may then be wrapped in his own tallit (see 4.2).

☐ Burial takes place as soon as possible after death. In practice this is likely to be within 24 hours. The funeral service itself is very brief. The mourners accompany the body on its last journey. During the short service at the graveside psalms from the Jewish Scriptures are chanted or intoned and the Kaddish prayer is recited:

Let the glory of God be extolled, let His great name be exalted in the world whose creation He willed. May His kingdom prevail, in our own day, in our own lives, and the life of all Israel. Let us say, Amen . . . May the source of peace send peace to all who mourn and comfort to all who are bereaved. Amen.

Working together, the mourners then begin to fill the grave with earth. By doing this, the people are both confirming in their own mind that the person is dead and showing their unity with the close relatives who are mourning.

The four stages of mourning

Judaism lays a strong emphasis upon the need to mourn. It sets out the four stages through which those who mourn should pass:

☐ The time between death and the funeral – during this time the mourner, known as an 'onan', is released from all other obligations;

☐ the week of mourning (shiva) that follows the funeral – during this time the mourners are expected to stay in their own homes and sit on the floor or low stools to receive visitors;

☐ a further period of 23 days during which life gradually returns to normal and the mourner is expected to assume slowly his or her ordinary responsibilities;

☐ a period of light mourning which lasts until the end of the 11th month after the person's death. A memorial or tombstone can be set up at any time after the earth has settled on the grave although, in Britain, some wait for at least a year before doing this. The tombstone is unveiled at a special ceremony.

Key question   How does the Jewish community deal with death and mourning?

The last prayer

My God and the God of my fathers, accept this prayer; do not ignore my supplication. Forgive me all the sins I have committed in my life-time and may it be your will to heal me. Yet, if you have decreed that I should die . . . may my death atone for all my sins and transgressions which I have committed before you . . . Grant me a share in the life to come . . . into your hands I commend my spirit. You have redeemed me, O Lord God of Truth. Hear, O Israel! the Lord our God, the Lord is one! The Lord, He is God, the Lord, He is God.

(Jewish Prayer Book)

☐ Explain, in your own words, what you think is meant by the words: 'Yet, if you have decreed that I should die . . . may my death atone for all my sins and transgressions which I have committed before you.'

Work to do

At a Jewish funeral mourners throw soil into the grave after the body has been placed in it.

(a) Why do you think that all the mourners are expected to take part in this?

(b) Can you think of *three* ways in which a Jewish funeral is different from that conducted in a religion you know about?

(c) Orthodox Jews insist on burying, and not cremating, their dead. Can you think of any reason for this?

(d) There are four stages of mourning through which a Jewish person is expected to pass. Why do you think that mourning is organised in this way? Do you think that it is a good idea to have these recognised stages of mourning?

Key words   **chevra kadisha:** 'holy society' – a voluntary body drawn from members of each synagogue. Among the tasks of this group is the cleansing of the dead body and its preparation for burial

PART 2

CHRISTIANITY

6. ORIGINS AND GROWTH

6.1 Who are the Christians?

Focusing questions
- What unites all Christians?
- How do Christians differ from one another?
- Which is the largest Christian denomination?

It is now about 2,000 years since **Jesus Christ** died. In that time the Christian religion has spread to almost every country in the world. **Christians** are people who: base their lives upon the example and teachings of Jesus of Nazareth; share a common core of beliefs with each other; apply common principles to their ways of worshipping and expressing their religious faith.

The variety that is Christianity

Throughout the world there are thought to be some 1,500,000,000 Christian believers. That figure makes Christianity the largest of all religions.
Of this number: around 900,000,000 belong to the **Roman Catholic Church** and around 600,000,000 belong to the various **Protestant** and **Orthodox churches**.

Amazingly, the number of different Christian Churches or denominations (see 7.1) is about 21,500. The variety that these various groupings bring to their religious worship is quite bewildering. Anyone, for instance, visiting a Zulu church in Africa, a Russian Orthodox church in Moscow, a parish church in rural East Anglia or a West Indian Christian community in London's East End would begin to appreciate the wide diversity of religious worship that is found under the Christian umbrella.

A Roman Catholic Mass.

The various Christian Churches organise themselves differently. Roman Catholic and Anglican (see 7.4) Churches are led by **bishops** and **priests** whilst some Churches do not have either. No single person, for example, is responsible for leading the worship in a **Quaker** community. The Quakers, incidentally, come together in a meeting house for their worship whilst the majority of Christians worship in a church. Just to confuse the issue further, though, the **Salvation Army** worships in a citadel whilst smaller Protestant Churches meet in chapels.

The central Christian service is that at which the people remember the death of Jesus Christ. Both Roman Catholics and Anglicans hold this service at least weekly and call it the **Eucharist**. Other denominations, such as the Baptists, usually hold the service monthly whilst two denominations, the Quakers and the Salvation Army, do not hold it at all. What is more, most Christian Churches have their own name for this service.

The tie that binds

What, then, is the link that binds all of these different groups together under the label 'Christian'? The common focus is their loyalty to a man who lived and taught on earth, who they believe was put to death and brought back to life by God: Jesus of Nazareth.

Key words

bishop: the highest of the three orders of ministry in a Church – the others being priest and deacon

Christian: any person who orders and directs their life by the teaching and example of Jesus of Nazareth. Such people are likely to be members of the Christian Church

Eucharist: central service in many Churches in which the death and resurrection of Jesus Christ are remembered and celebrated

Jesus Christ: born around 4 BCE in Bethlehem of Judea. Christ is the title he was given and means 'Anointed One'

Orthodox Church: a number of self-governing Churches found mainly in Eastern Europe

priest: person who has been given the authority, in the Anglican and Roman Catholic Churches, to lead public worship and administer the sacraments – women priests are only to be found in some Anglican Churches

Protestant Church: Church whose members are Christian, but owe no allegiance to either the Roman Catholic or Orthodox Churches

Quakers: or Society of Friends – Christian denomination begun in the 17th century through the preaching of George Fox

Roman Catholic Church: the worldwide body of Christians who owe their allegiance to the Pope in Rome

Salvation Army: Protestant denomination started in 1880 by Catherine and William Booth

6.2 Jesus of Nazareth

Focusing questions

■ Why is it difficult to piece together an outline of the life of Jesus?
■ Into which country was Jesus born and who controlled it at the time?
■ What was the main theme of the teaching of Jesus?
■ How did Jesus meet his death and what happened three days later?

There is little doubt that the man, Jesus of Nazareth, lived 2,000 years ago in the country that is now called Israel. It is equally clear that any attempt to reconstruct a detailed and accurate picture of his childhood, life, teaching, death and resurrection presents tremendous problems.

Apart from one or two brief references to Jesus from Jewish and Roman historians of the time the only record that we have of him is found in the four **Gospels** in the New Testament. The first of these, Mark, was not written until some 40 years after Jesus died. There was a gap of at least 60 years after his death before the last Gospel, John, saw the light of day.

There are some Christians who accept every word written in the Bible as the literal truth. These people are called **fundamentalists** and they are found in every branch of the Christian Church. Others believe that the teachings and claims of Jesus are often open to several different interpretations and so must be judged carefully. Most Christians, however, do find a broad measure of agreement on the outline of the life of Jesus of Nazareth.

The birth of Jesus

The country into which Jesus was born had been under Roman occupation for a long time when an unmarried Jewish couple, Joseph and Mary, received the startling news that they were to be the parents of a son called Jesus. For centuries the Jewish nation had looked forward to the coming of a Messiah, and God's messenger, in announcing the coming birth to Mary and Joseph, made it quite clear that Jesus was to be that Messiah.

The work of Jesus

After being baptised by John the Baptist in the River Jordan, Jesus, at the age of thirty, began a public ministry which lasted for only about three years. He began by choosing twelve **disciples** with whom he was to share the rest of his life and who were to continue his work after he died. There are many occasions in the Gospels where Jesus is reported as exercising extraordinary power over evil – casting out demons, healing the sick, restoring sight to the blind, calming raging storms and feeding those who were hungry.

The teaching of Jesus

Apart from performing many miracles Jesus also went through Israel teaching his disciples and the crowds of ordinary people about the coming of the **kingdom of God**. He stressed that those who would enter this kingdom would not be those who held religious office, but those who believed in the word of God, even if they were considered to be outcasts – for example, the poor, the tax-collectors and the prostitutes. Much of this teaching was given in the form of **parables**.

Crucifixion and Resurrection

From the very beginning of his public work Jesus's behaviour and teaching upset the religious leaders of the time. They conspired together to bring about his death, taking him before the Roman governor of the province, **Pontius Pilate**, whom they persuaded to have Jesus executed. A large proportion of the material about Jesus in the Gospels is concerned with the last week in his life. The same Gospels also carry extended accounts of the return to life (the Resurrection – see 10.4) of Jesus three days later.

Christians draw much of their inspiration and motivation to live the Christian life in the modern world from this life-story.

Key question **What were the most important aspects of the life and teaching of Jesus of Nazareth?**

Work to do

1. Find out more about Jesus by looking up these references and making your own notes on them:

    (a) The birth of Jesus. Luke 2.1–20.

    (b) Jesus begins his public ministry. Mark 1.

    (c) The teachings of Jesus. Matthew 5, 6 and 7.

    (d) Parables of Jesus. Luke 8.1–15; 14.15–24; 15.11–32.

    (e) Miracles of Jesus. Matthew 8.28–34; 9.18–34.

    (f) The death of Jesus. Mark 14, 15.

    (g) The resurrection of Jesus. Mark 16.1–8.

A scene from 'Jesus Christ Superstar'.

2. The photo shows how a modern musical portrays Jesus. What kind of a figure do you think he was?

Key words   **disciple:** one who follows the teaching of any leader – one of Jesus's personal followers, soon to become known as 'Apostles'

fundamentalist: a Christian who believes, amongst other things, that the Bible is literally true

Gospel: the word means 'good news' and there are four Gospels in the New Testament – Matthew, Mark, Luke and John

kingdom of God: the spiritual kingdom over which God would rule

parable: a short story which has some kind of spiritual significance or teaching

Pontius Pilate: the Roman governor of Judea from 26 CE to 36 CE

6.3 Understanding Jesus of Nazareth

Focusing questions
- ■ **What is the Incarnation?**
- ■ **What is the Atonement?**
- ■ **What do Christians hope for in the future?**

The life-story of Jesus is very important to all Christians but so too are the beliefs about him conveyed both through this life-story and through the regular worship of the Christian community. Such religious acts as prayers, sermons and singing hymns all gain their real power from the way that they combine the life-story of Jesus with the beliefs that Christians hold about him. Behind these beliefs lies a very long history, during which Christians of all kinds have reflected on the meaning of Jesus's life and what is involved in believing that he was 'God in human flesh'.

Christians hold the following beliefs about Jesus of Nazareth:

- ☐ Jesus was God's only Son. In Mark's description of the baptism of Jesus a voice from heaven tells him: 'You are my Son, whom I love; with you I am well pleased.' The belief that Jesus was God's Son runs through all of the Gospels.
- ☐ Jesus was conceived in the womb of Mary by the power of the **Holy Spirit**. There is debate amongst Christians today about the **Virgin Birth**. Was Jesus conceived in the normal way or was he conceived by a supernatural operation of God's Spirit? On this question Christians disagree. The important thing, though, is not how Jesus was born but that Jesus was God in human form (the **Incarnation**).
- ☐ Jesus grew up, taught and ministered to the needs of people in the country of Palestine. His earthly life lasted little more than 30 years.
- ☐ Jesus was tried, crucified and buried during the time that Pontius Pilate was procurator of Judaea. Christians do not believe that this death was coincidental or a mistake. They understand it as part of God's plan to bring mankind back to Himself (the **Atonement**).
- ☐ Jesus came back to life and ascended into heaven. It was only after this happened that the Holy Spirit was given to the Christian Church. Several centuries after the time of Jesus, Christians set out their belief in God as the **Trinity** – God the Father, God the Son and God the Holy Spirit. (You can find out more about this belief in 8.1.)
- ☐ Jesus will return to the earth at some future time to set up God's kingdom on earth. The early Christians expected this to happen during their lifetime and there is every reason to think that Jesus expected it to happen soon as well. It remains the hope, however, of many Christians that Jesus will return to this earth at a time known only to God.

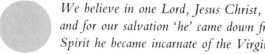

Key question **What do Christians believe about Jesus?**

The **Nicene Creed** is one of the earliest known statements of Christian belief. Read this extract from it:

We believe in one Lord, Jesus Christ, the only Son of God . . . For us men and for our salvation 'he' came down from heaven; by the power of the Holy Spirit he became incarnate of the Virgin Mary, and was made man. For our sake he was crucified under Pontius Pilate; he suffered and was buried. On the third day he rose again in accordance with the scriptures; he ascended into heaven, and is seated on the right hand of the Father. He will come in glory to judge the quick and the dead, and his kingdom will have no end.

☐ This creed makes many statments of belief about Jesus. Make a list of them.

A Nicaraguan representation of the Crucifixion.

Work to do

1. Can you try to explain, in your own words, what each of these words or phrases means:

    (a) The Incarnation

    (b) The Virgin Birth

    (c) The Trinity

    (d) The Atonement

2. Read this extract from Matthew's Gospel:

    'But what about you?' 'Jesus asked his disciples' 'Who do you say I am?' Simon Peter answered, 'You are the Christ, the Son of the living God.'

Look up the full account of this episode in Matthew 16.13–28 to find out the occasion when this declaration was made and the response of Jesus to it.

Key words   **Atonement:** the belief that the world has been forgiven for its sins through the death of Jesus

Holy Spirit: the third person in the Trinity – believed to be God present and active in the world

Incarnation: the belief that Jesus was God and yet became a full human being

Nicene Creed: one of the earliest statements of Christian belief thought to have been first drawn up by the Council of Nicea in 325 CE

Trinity: the belief that God is three persons – Father, Son and Holy Spirit

Virgin Birth: belief held by many Christians that Mary was a virgin when she was impregnated by the Holy Spirit

6.4 The Church is born

Focusing questions

- What happened to the Christian disciples on the day of Pentecost?
- What were the roles of Peter and Paul in the expansion of the early Christian Church?
- Who was the first Christian Roman emperor and why was he converted?

Most of our knowledge about the early Christian Church comes from the New Testament and, in particular, from the **Acts of the Apostles**. As far as we know, this book was written towards the end of the 1st century by **Luke**, who also wrote one of the Gospels. In fact, there is good reason to think that Luke set out to write a two-part history of the beginnings of the Christian faith.

The festival of Pentecost

Pentecost is a Jewish harvest festival (Shavuot – see 3.7), held 50 days after the great feast of Passover. In Roman times Jews would converge on the city of Jerusalem from all over the Empire to celebrate the giving of their precious law (Torah) to Moses on Mount Sinai. According to the Acts of the Apostles, it was in the middle of this great crowd of people that the disciples underwent an experience which transformed them. Luke, like other writers in the New Testament, was not writing 'history' in our sense of the word. He was writing to persuade others to believe in Jesus. We do not, therefore, know precisely what happened, but it is clear that from this point on these first Christians believed that they were called to preach about Jesus of Nazareth, under the inspiration of God and through the power of God's Spirit. Luke tells us that the impact of their preaching upon the people was so great that every day new converts were added to the young Church. It was in Jerusalem that the Christian Church was born.

The message spreads

To begin with, the leader of this Christian community was **Peter**, who, according to Jesus's promise, was to be the rock upon which the early Church would be built. He undertook preaching tours but, as a Jew, seemed unable to accept that non-Jews (Gentiles) should be welcomed into the Church as equal partners. After a time, he was superseded by **Paul**, who, before his conversion, had ruthlessly persecuted the Christians. He was to become a tireless worker and letter-writer in the Christian cause. He made three missionary journeys to the various parts of the Roman Empire and was probably put to death by the Emperor Nero in the same persecution that also claimed the life of Peter (in about 65 CE).

During these early years the Christians either worshipped in the Jewish synagogues or, later, in each other's homes. It was to be several centuries before churches were specially built. During this time there were many periods of persecution but the Church survived. Soon a quite elaborate organisation grew up with bishops being appointed to look after the groups of Christians that were springing up everywhere.

The situation for the Christian Church changed dramatically when the Roman Emperor **Constantine** became a Christian and declared Christianity to be the official religion of his empire. This came about because the emperor believed his victory in an important battle (Milvian Bridge in 312) had been due to the intervention of the Christian God.

Key question **How was the Christian Church born and what kind of impact did it have on the Roman Empire?**

> *Jesus speaks to Peter: 'And I tell you that you are Peter, and on this*
> *rock I will build my church, and the gates of Hades will not overcome it.*
> *I will give you the keys of the kingdom of heaven . . .'*
> **(Matthew 16.18,19)**

☐ Can you find out which Church claims to be directly descended from Peter's?

☐ What importance does this have for the Church today?

Work to do

1. Read Acts 2.1–5. Does the passage strike you as being a 'literal' description of what happened on the Day of Pentecost, or a 'poetic' attempt to describe some supernatural event?

2. Read Acts 5.17–42, 6.8–7.60 and 8.1–3 before trying to answer these questions:

(a) Who was the first Christian martyr and why was he put to death?

(b) Why was the Christian Church persecuted so often in its early life?

(c) Find out as much as you can about *one* group of people who have been persecuted in the 20th century.

Key words   **Acts of the Apostles:** book in the New Testament which tells the story of the Christian Church from the time of the resurrection of Jesus to the missionary journeys of Paul

Constantine: 274–337) the first Christian Roman emperor

Luke: a doctor and companion of Paul regarded as the author of the Gospel bearing his name and of the Acts of the Apostles

Paul: the leading figure in the early Christian community, responsible for much of its missionary work

Pentecost: Jewish festival of Shavuot, which falls 50 days after Passover; the day on which the Christian disciples were given the Holy Spirit

Peter: the name means 'rock' and was given to Simon, one of the disciples of Jesus

6.5 Milestones in Church history

Focusing questions

- How was the Christian message first brought to Britain?
- What was the Inquisition?
- What was the Reformation?

There is still an active Christian community on Iona. Can you find this island on a map?

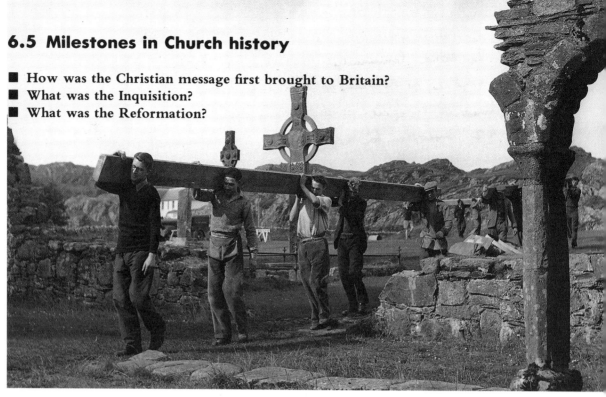

The early Christian Church in the British Isles

It seems that the Christian message was first brought to England by traders and Roman soldiers who were posted to Britain. The first Christian Roman soldier known to us by name is Alban, who was beheaded outside the town of Verulamium early in the 3rd century CE for hiding a Christian priest. Almost two hundred years later, **St Patrick** escaped from being a slave in Ireland, trained to be a priest in England, then returned to Ireland in 431. He built many churches and monasteries there, turning Ireland into a centre of Christianity.

Indeed, it was from Ireland that a whole succession of Christian missionaries were to sail in the following years. Amongst them was Columba, who, with twelve friends, sailed to the island of Iona, off the coast of Scotland. From there he spread the Gospel through western Scotland and Northumbria. Some time later, in 635, a monk from Iona, Aidan, founded a monastery at Lindisfarne, off the Northumberland coast.

In 597 Pope Gregory I sent a monk called **Augustine** to convert the English, but when he landed in Kent he was surprised to find a sizeable Christian Church already established. His preaching, though, did result in the conversion to Christianity of King Ethelbert. The king's gift of land to Augustine resulted in the building of the first cathedral at Canterbury and the enthronement of Augustine as its archbishop.

The Great Schism and the Inquisition

The Great Schism, which took place in 1054, saw the division of the Christian Church into two halves – East and West. You can find out more about this in 7.1. The western branch of the Church was further disturbed when in 1233 Pope Gregory IX initiated the **Inquisition**. The Inquisition authorised the use of torture against those suspected of being **heretics**. Offenders were tried before Church courts and, if found guilty, could be fined, imprisoned for life or even burnt at the stake.

The Reformation

During the 16th century two Continental churchmen, Martin Luther and John Calvin, set out to reform the Roman Catholic Church. When the Catholic Church refused to accept the demands of the Reformers, as its critics were called, various Protestant denominations outside the Catholic Church were formed.

Protestant Churches in England

In 1534 King Henry VIII declared himself to be the head of a new Protestant Church of England, replacing the Pope (see 7.4). Before long several other Protestant denominations were to come into existence.

Baptist Churches (at first called Anabaptist Churches) began to be formed in the 16th century, the Methodist Church was formed by John Wesley in the 18th century and the Salvation Army was founded in the 19th century.

The Christian Church in the 20th century

During the 20th century many important events have taken place. Two of particular importance are:

☐ The formation of the **World Council of Churches** in 1948, which was the most serious attempt yet to bring all Churches, large and small, together;
☐ The **Second Vatican Council**, which met between 1962 and 1965, as an attempt to 'let some fresh air into the Roman Catholic Church' (see 7.3).

Key question **What has happened to the Christian Church since its days in the Roman Empire?**

Work to do

1. Several Christian groups or denominations have been mentioned in this unit. Try to find out about the activities in your district or town of *two* of the following: (a) the Methodists; (b) the Baptists; (c) the Salvation Army; (d) the Quakers.

2. Find out as much as you can about Martin Luther, John Calvin and the other Reformers. Why were the followers of Martin Luther called 'Protestants'?

Key words **Augustine:** sent to England in 597; the first Archbishop of Canterbury

heretic: person who rejects all or part of a Church's doctrine

Inquisition: a special institution set up by the Roman Catholic Church to suppress heretics

Patrick: (389–461) the man who brought Christianity to Ireland – now its patron saint

Second Vatican Council: set up by Pope John XXIII in 1962 to reform the Roman Catholic Church

World Council of Churches: the organisation set up in 1948 to unite the main Christian Churches

7. ONE CHURCH – MANY CHURCHES

7.1 Three branches of the one Church

Focusing questions
- What are the names of the three branches of the Christian Church?
- What was the Great Schism?
- Who are the Nonconformists?

The Christian Church began its life as a small off-shoot of Judaism in the country called Palestine, but it soon spread throughout the Roman Empire and beyond. Over the centuries that followed it broke up into a number of different **denominations** or Churches. These denominations fall into three broad groups:

- ☐ the Orthodox Church;
- ☐ the Protestant Church;
- ☐ the Roman Catholic Church.

From the map you can see where each of these three Churches is most securely established today.

The three branches of the Christian Church.

The Great Schism

The church remained united until 1054, when a doctrinal disagreement caused it to separate into two halves. This division came to be called the Great Schism. The eastern part of the Church became known as the Orthodox Church whilst the western section became the Roman Catholic Church. Despite many attempts to heal the breach these two Churches remain separated today, although there are many close similarities in their beliefs and forms of worship.

The Reformation

As we saw in 6.5 a protest sprang up in the 16th century against the power and corruption of the Catholic Church. This was known as the Reformation and those who supported this protest were called Protestants ('those who protest'). Protestants refused to accept the authority of the **Pope** in Rome, preferring to seek God's guidance through reading the Bible. In England, under Henry VIII, the Protestants broke away from the Catholic Church to form the **Church of England** (also known as the Anglican Church). The Act of Supremacy, passed in 1534, made the monarch the head of the Church of England instead of the Pope. From the very beginning the Church of England received many privileges and so became the **Established Church**. The same is still true today.

As time went on, however, many English Christians grew dissatisfied with the Church of England. Some of them wanted to carry their 'protest' further and out of their number various **Nonconformist** Churches grew up. Since the 17th century such denominations as the Quakers, the Methodists, the Baptists and the Salvation Army have become an integral part of Church life in England and elsewhere.

A Greek Orthodox service in Bethlehem.

Key question   **Why are there three main branches of the Christian Church?**

Work to do

1. Find out as much as you can about *one* of the following:
   (a) the Roman Catholic Church;
   (b) the Orthodox Church;
   (c) the Church of England.

2. The Church of England contains many different groups of Christian believers. Some people maintain that this is a weakness and that all members should think and worship in the same way. Others insist that the Church of England should accept a variety of beliefs. What do you think?

Key words   **Church of England:** the main Church in England – brought into existence by Henry VIII

denomination: a group within, or a branch of, the Christian Church

Established Church: a Church which enjoys certain privileges and carries some responsibilities

Nonconformist: a term to describe those Churches or people who are Protestant, but not members of the Church of England

Pope: the Bishop of Rome – the supreme authority in the Catholic Church

7.2 The Orthodox Churches

Focusing questions
- What does the word 'Orthodox' mean?
- What issue caused a split in the Orthodox Church in the 6th century?
- What is the central service of the Orthodox Church?
- What beliefs do all Orthodox Christians have in common?

Of all the main Christian groupings the one about which most people in Britain know least is the Orthodox Church. This is despite the fact that there are about 130,000,000 Orthodox Christians scattered throughout the world, most of whom are to be found in Eastern Europe. The Orthodox Church is made up of two 'families', the Eastern Orthodox and the Oriental Orthodox Churches.

Eastern Orthodox Church

About 20 different Orthodox Churches belong to the Eastern Orthodox Church. All of these accept the authority of the Ecumenical Patriarch of Constantinople, who lives in Istanbul. Amongst this 'family' are the Russian, Romanian, Bulgarian, Serbian, Georgian and Greek Orthodox Churches, which claim between them a membership of over 100,000,000 people.

Oriental Orthodox Church

This, the smaller 'family', includes the Coptic, Syrian and Ethiopian Orthodox Churches. Altogether there are about 30,000,000 people in this branch of the Orthodox Church.

An early disagreement

It was in the 6th century CE that these two groups split from each other. They disagreed over whether Jesus had two natures – divine and human – or just one. Today, although the two Churches have reached an agreement over this issue, they remain separate from each other. Apart from minor differences, however, their beliefs and styles of worship are very similar.

The beliefs of the Orthodox Church

Three beliefs, in particular, unite all Orthodox Christians.

☐ They believe that God is a Trinity – Father, Son and Holy Spirit. The word 'Orthodox' has been created from two Greek words: orthos (rightly) and doxa (belief). Orthodox Christians, therefore, see themselves as those who 'rightly believe in God'. They have done this by using the **doxology**: 'Glory to the Father and to the Son and to the Holy Spirit.'
☐ Orthodox Christians believe that the second person of the Trinity – Jesus Christ – came to earth and lived a normal human life. He was fully God and fully man.
☐ They believe that the Church is the body of Christ. The Church has been established by God and is His visible form on earth.

Orthodox worship

Orthodox churches are usually square, domed buildings. The square represents correctness and equality, allowing people to feel equal before God. The dome represents the universe, whilst the floor represents the earth. The four corners of the building remind worshippers of the four Gospels.

Central to Orthodox worship is the very beautiful service of Holy Communion or **Liturgy**. For Orthodox Christians this 'eternal liturgy' is a window into heaven. Through it they are able to see God the Father, God the Son and God the Holy Spirit.

Orthodox Christians believe that God is all-powerful and beyond human understanding. For this reason, they use **icons** to worship Him. Icons, which may be found in both public and private places, are believed to be copies of particular heavenly images. They are treated with the greatest possible respect by believers but they are not worshipped in themselves. They are 'aids' designed to help the worshipper to worship God.

Key question **What beliefs are distinctive to the Orthodox Church and how are these reflected in their places of worship?**

> ### Work to do
> In this photograph you can see a priest of the Coptic Church in Ethiopia.
> (a) Find out how Christianity came to Ethiopia.
> (b) Name *two* beliefs which all Orthodox Christians hold in common.

A Coptic priest in Ethiopia.

Key words **doxology:** set form of words praising God

icons: paintings of saints or members of the Holy Family which are used in the Orthodox Church as an aid to worship

Liturgy: name applied within the Orthodox Church to the service of Holy Communion – more generally, the term 'liturgy' means any form of public worship

7.3 The Roman Catholic Church

Focusing questions

- Who is the head of the Roman Catholic Church and how much authority does he have?
- Which council was called to update the Church and who called it?
- What changes were made as a result of that council?

As a separate branch of the Christian Church the Roman Catholic Church has expanded so rapidly that six out of every ten Christians are now Roman Catholics. You will find members of this Church in every continent, but it is in Latin America, Africa, and Europe that it is particularly strong.

The Pope

Roman Catholics believe that St Peter was the first Bishop of Rome and that Jesus gave the keys of the kingdom of God to him. They claim that most of their beliefs go back to Peter and have been handed on to each successive Pope by the 'laying on of hands'. The present Pope, John Paul II, was elected in 1978 and is the 275th man to hold the position.

The Pope has the power to proclaim new doctrines for the Church whenever he speaks 'infallibly' or **ex cathedra**. Such new beliefs must then be held by all Catholics. The following beliefs concerning the **Virgin Mary**, for example, have been proclaimed in the last two centuries: that Mary had been born 'without sin' (the Immaculate Conception); that Mary was carried up into heaven at the end of her life without dying (the Bodily Assumption).

A Chinese sculpture of the Madonna and child. Why is Mary so important in the Roman Catholic Church?

The Second Vatican Council

A very important milestone in the life of the Roman Catholic Church was passed in 1870 when all of the Church's **cardinals** and bishops took part in the First Vatican Council. A very popular Pope, John XXIII (1958–63), called a Second Vatican Council between 1962 and 1965 to 'Open the windows and let the wind of change blow through the Church'.

This council has had a considerable effect upon the Roman Catholic Church. Amongst many statements it declared the following:

☐ Nothing can replace the importance of prayer, worship and the **sacraments** in the life of the Church. Protestants only recognise two sacraments – baptism and Holy Communion (which Catholics call the **Mass**). The Roman Catholic Church adds five more – confirmation, penance, marriage, ordination to the priesthood and anointing the dying with oil.

74

☐ The old Latin Mass should be replaced by a service in the language of the congregation, with new prayers and music. The worshippers should be encouraged to play an important part in this and other services.

☐ The Pope should share responsibility for running the Church with the cardinals, bishops, clergy and ordinary church members.

☐ The Roman Catholic Church should forge new links with members of other Christian denominations, those of other religious faiths and those with no faith at all.

☐ Roman Catholics should rethink their attitude to such important matters as birth-control, abortion and euthanasia.

☐ The Roman Catholic Church should support the struggle of the poor for a better standard of living.

Some of these recommendations have been put into effect. The Mass, for instance, is now conducted in the language of the congregation and is not usually said in Latin any more. On the other hand, the attitude of the Catholic Church towards birth-control, abortion and euthanasia has not changed. In fact, it has hardened considerably since the Second Vatican Council.

Key question **What is distinctive about the beliefs and worship of the Roman Catholic Church?**

Work to do

In this extract a bishop who attended the Second Vatican Council is speaking about the effect that it had upon him:

When I heard that Pope John XXIII had called a council in the Vatican I was very doubtful about it. It had been almost a century since the last one and I didn't think that it would accomplish much. In the event, it was to be the most amazing spiritual experience with effects that are still being felt in the Roman Catholic Church today.

(a) When had the previous Vatican Council been held?

(b) What did Pope John XXIII say would be the purpose of the Second Vatican Council?

(c) What did the Second Vatican Council say about:
   – the Mass;
   – birth-control, euthanasia and abortion;
   – the running of the Church?

Key words **cardinal:** a holder of the highest office in the Roman Catholic Church apart from that of Pope, who is elected by the cardinals

ex cathedra: literally 'from the throne' – when the Pope makes a statement 'ex cathedra' he is speaking with all the authority of God and his words must be accepted by all Catholics

Mass: the term used for the Eucharist or Lord's Supper by Roman Catholics

sacrament: religious ceremony regarded as an outward, physical sign of an inward, spiritual blessing

Virgin Mary: the mother of Jesus – a very important figure in Roman Catholic belief and worship

7.4 The Church of England

Focusing questions

- How did the Church of England first come into existence?
- What does it mean to be the 'Established Church'?
- What do most Anglicans believe?

When the monk Augustine arrived in England, in 597, to convert the 'heathen English' he found, much to his surprise, a flourishing Church (see 6.5). After some initial reluctance this Church was persuaded to give its allegiance to the Pope in Rome. Over the passage of time this relationship caused many problems, and matters came to a head in the 16th century.

Henry VIII and the Church in England

Because he was the head of the Church, the Pope alone could grant the necessary permission to dissolve a marriage. When Henry VIII applied to have his first marriage dissolved he was refused, so he chose to break the English Church's link with Rome, declaring himself to be its 'Especial Protector, only and supreme lord, and, as far as the law of Christ allows, even supreme head of the Church'.

The power of the Pope over the Church of England was finally broken when, in 1536 and 1539, two Acts of Dissolution allowed the monasteries to be dissolved. In 1538 a copy of the Great Bible, translated from the Latin, was placed in every parish church in the country. The effects of making the Bible available to the people in their own language were considerable. So was the work of **Thomas Cranmer**, who became Archbishop of Canterbury under Henry. Cranmer was the genius behind the **Book of Common Prayer** which is still used in many Church services. Cranmer was put to death in the reign of Mary, a zealous Catholic, but the Church of England was by now so well established that Elizabeth I took the title 'Supreme Governor of the Church of England'.

What do Anglicans believe?

Members of the Church of England (Anglicans) can be found throughout the world today. Canterbury Cathedral, founded by Augustine, is their mother church and the Archbishop of Canterbury their 'unofficial' leader. In practice, the Church of England has divided itself into three broad groups of believers:

- ☐ The High Church, or Anglo-Catholics, who in their belief and worship are closest to the Roman Catholic Church. They place a heavy emphasis upon ritual and ceremony.
- ☐ The Low Church, or Evangelicals, who believe strongly in the Bible, personal conversion to Christ and sharing their faith with others.
- ☐ The Broad Church, whose outlook lies between those of the Anglo-Catholic and Evangelical Anglicans, emphasises openness in belief and worship.

To this day the Church of England enjoys a privileged position in Britain. The sovereign must belong to this Church since he or she is its head and promises, when crowned, to protect it. The actual coronation of the monarch is carried out by the Archbishop of Canterbury. The two archbishops of the Church of England together with 24 bishops have seats in the House of Lords. This is a privilege which is not extended to any other Church.

Key question What is distinctive about the Church of England?

What is an Anglican?

All Anglicans should hold these four beliefs:

1. That the Holy Scriptures contain 'all things necessary for salvation'.

2. That the **creeds** *contain all that Anglicans should believe (see 8.3).*

3. That the two sacraments of baptism and Holy Communion should be celebrated using the actual words of Christ, as recorded in the Bible.

4. That bishops are appointed to lead the Church although the line of bishops cannot be traced back through Peter to Christ.

(Records of the Lambeth Conference, 1888)

☐ Draw up a list of some of the things that Roman Catholics believe and another of things Anglicans believe. Are there any areas of belief which overlap?

Work to do

1. Look at this photograph carefully:

(a) What do you think is happening?

(b) Where do you think that the ceremony is taking place?

(c) How do you know the ceremony is not taking place in a church of another denomination?

2. The Church of England is called the 'Established Church'.

(a) What do you think this means?

(b) What are *two* advantages and *two* disadvantages of the Church being established?

Key words   **Book of Common Prayer:** book containing all of the recognised services for use in the Church of England

Thomas Cranmer: Henry VIII's Archbishop of Canterbury, he was largely responsible for writing the Book of Common Prayer and was put to death by Queen Mary

creed: a formal statement of religious belief

7.5 The Nonconformists

Focusing questions

- What is distinctive about the Presbyterians?
- Who founded the Quakers and for what reason?
- Which distinctive belief is held by Baptists?
- Who founded the Methodists and how did they receive their name?

It was not long after the Reformation that the Protestant Church began to split into many denominations. A Nonconformist (see 7.1) is any Protestant who does not belong to the Church of England.

The Presbyterians

The **Presbyterian** Church closely follows the form of Church government laid down by John Calvin, the Reformer. It emphasises:

- [ ] the authority of the Bible;
- [ ] the importance of the local congregation;
- [ ] simple Church worship based upon readings from the Bible, hymns, spoken prayers by the minister and a sermon on a biblical passage.

Presbyterian churches are normally simple both inside and out.

The Quakers (Society of Friends)

The founder of this denomination, George Fox, wanted his followers to return to the faith and simple life-style of the early Christians. He called his denomination the 'Society of Friends' because he wanted his followers to be Friends of Christ and of each other. They were called 'Quakers' by a judge who at Fox's trial in 1650 was told by Fox to 'Tremble at the voice of the Lord'.

The Baptists

In the 17th century many Churches came into being which were opposed to the practice of baptising children. They insisted that only adults who trusted in Christ could be properly baptised. These '**Baptists**' were persecuted in the 17th century but have now become a large and world-wide movement with some 40,000,000 members.

The Methodists

It was the English preacher, John Wesley, who founded **Methodism**. The name was first applied when Wesley was studying at Oxford, because of the methodical way in which he read and studied the Bible. He had been a minister of the Church of England but had a spiritual experience which convinced him that God had taken away his sins. He travelled the length and breadth of England on horseback preaching to immense crowds and founding many churches.

The Salvation Army

The Salvation Army is an organisation which was founded in 1877 by Catherine and William Booth. They had as a major aim the conversion of the poor and the social outcasts to Christianity. The new movement they formed was organised along military lines. The Army continues to pour immense amounts of energy and money into running open-air meetings, helping released prisoners, searching for missing persons and other practical, social work.

What are the main Nonconformist groups and what is their distinctive contribution to the Christian Church?

Work to do
You will need to carry out some research before you try to answer these questions:
  (a) Which features would you be likely to find in an Anglican church but not in a Nonconformist church?
  (b) Which features would you be likely to find in a Roman Catholic church but not in a Nonconformist church?
  (c) Which feature is found in a Baptist church but not in other Nonconformist churches?
  (d) What is the distinctive feature inside most Salvation Army citadels?

Key words

Baptists: members of the world-wide Protestant denomination committed to the baptism of adults, rather than children, and to the authority of the Bible as the Word of God

Methodism: Protestant denomination which came into being through the preaching of John Wesley (1703–91)

Presbyterians: early Nonconformist denomination which believes that presbyters (or elders) should lead each church

A Salvation Army service. What are the people wearing?

8. WHAT DO CHRISTIANS BELIEVE?

8.1 What do Christians believe about the Trinity?

Focusing questions

- ■ What is the Trinity in Christian belief?
- ■ What do Christians believe about God?
- ■ What do Christians believe about Jesus Christ?
- ■ What do Christians believe about the Holy Spirit?

Christians believe that there is one God who has revealed Himself to mankind in three different ways, as God the Father, as Jesus Christ and as the Holy Spirit.

God as the Father

From its opening words

In the beginning God created the heaven and the earth

through to the teaching of Jesus the Bible teaches certain important truths about God:

- ☐ God is the creator of all that exists – the universe, the world, nature and mankind. Nothing exists that has not been brought into being by God.
- ☐ God is the Father of all living things. Just as a human father cares for his children so God cares for the whole of creation and especially the human beings, who are responsible, under God, for looking after it.
- ☐ God is a personal being and not an abstract force that made the world and then left it totally alone. The Christian God is one who is deeply involved in the affairs of the world and all human beings.

God as Jesus Christ

Christians believe that God lived on earth in the person of Jesus Christ. As a human being he experienced all of the emotions associated with being human – he wept, pleaded, argued, was angry, suffered and died. Just as God is immortal, however, so Jesus was able to rise from the dead after three days. The only explanation that any Christian will offer for this is that it was God who brought Jesus back from the dead. At some future time Christians believe that Jesus will return to the earth, set up God's kingdom and judge all people.

God as Holy Spirit

Before he left the earth Jesus promised his disciples that he would always be with them. His physical presence, though, would be removed and replaced by his Spirit, who would act as their guide. As we saw in 6.4 this happened after the day of Pentecost.

The Trinity

What, then, do Christians mean when they speak of the Trinity? There are not *three* gods in Christianity (as the word 'Trinity' suggests) but only one. That God, however, the maker of heaven and earth, has shown Himself to man in *three* different ways – 'God the Father' sent 'God the Son' to earth and, after he left, 'God the Holy Spirit' continued God's work on earth.

Key question **What do Christians believe about God?**

Jesus is speaking about the Holy Spirit:

> *But when he, the Spirit of truth, comes, he will guide you into all truth. He will not speak on his own; he will speak only what he hears, and he will tell you what is yet to come.*
> **(John 16.13)**

☐ Why do you think that God's Holy Spirit is called 'the Spirit of truth'?

Work to do

1. Read the parable of the Prodigal Son told in Luke 15.11–31. Christians have always understood this to be a parable told by Jesus to help them to understand the fatherhood of God. If this is so, what qualities of a good father does it highlight and how does it help us to understand the Christian picture of God as Father?

2. Here are some quotations from the Bible about Jesus Christ.
(a) *But God raised him from the dead, freeing him from the agony of death.* (Acts 2.24)
(b) *For we are God's workmanship, created in Christ Jesus to do good works, which God prepared in advance for us to do.* (Ephesians 2.10)
(c) *Therefore God exalted him to the highest place and gave him the name that is above every name, that at the name of Jesus every knee should bow, in heaven and on earth and under the earth, and every tongue confess that Jesus Christ is Lord, to the glory of God the Father.* (Philippians 2.9–11)
What do these extracts tell us about Jesus Christ?

3. The following extracts are taken from two old Christian creeds.
(a) *We believe in one God, the Father Almighty, maker of heaven and earth, of all that is seen and unseen.*
(b) *I believe in God, the Father Almighty, Creator of the heaven and earth.*
These two extracts make four points about God. What are they?

8.2 What do Christians believe about the creeds?

Focusing questions
■ How were the earliest Christian 'creeds' formed?
■ How were the creeds used during baptismal services?
■ What are the three main Christian creeds?

The early creeds

Quite how most of the early creeds came into being we do not know. There is a legend, for example, that the twelve Apostles of Jesus came together and actually composed one of the earliest creeds – the Apostles' Creed – before setting out to the four corners of the earth to preach the Gospel. We now know that there is no truth behind the legend – it was just invented to give that particular creed as much authority as possible.

In fact, to discover the origins of the earliest creeds we have to go back to the **New Testament**. The early Christians used different forms of words to teach early converts about the Christian faith. The earliest of these formulae were about Jesus the Lord, but words about God the Father were soon to be added. One of the earliest 'catchwords' to become popular amongst the early Christians was: 'God, who has raised the Lord Jesus from the dead'.

In the earliest days these formulae of faith were only used within small communities, but as the Christians travelled more widely so their use spread. They were particularly useful in teaching people who came forward to offer themselves for baptism. For months beforehand the bishop 'handed out' the short statements, commenting on them phrase by phrase. Then, during the baptism itself, the converts were expected 'to give the creeds back' as their own personal commitment to Christ.

'The Resurrection', a painting by Stanley Spencer.

The fight against heresy

In the early centuries of the Christian Church three main creeds were produced:

The Apostles' Creed: little is known about this creed, which probably originated as early as the 2nd century CE. It is rarely used today.

The Nicene Creed is the most widely used Christian creed today although many Churches have written their own modern creed. The Nicene Creed first saw the light of day in 325 (at the Council of Nicaea) and was later refined at the Council of Constantinople in 381 CE. Both of these councils were concerned to rebut **heresy** and restate what orthodox Christians should believe.

The Athanasian Creed started life in the middle of the 4th century but was too lengthy to become popular. It does, however, start with words which underline just why the creeds were drawn up in the first place:

> Whosoever will be saved: before all things it is necessary that he hold the Catholic Faith. Which Faith except everyone do keep whole and undefiled; without doubt he shall perish everlastingly.

The creeds were intended to spell out that very 'Catholic (or universal) Faith'.

Key question   **How have creeds been used by Christians through the centuries?**

St Hippolytus, in about 215 CE, speaks of those being baptised:

> And when he who is to be baptised goes down to the water, let him who baptises lay hands on him saying thus, 'Dost thou believe in God the Father almighty?' And he who is being baptised shall say, 'I believe.' Let him forthwith baptise him once, having his hand laid upon his head. And after this let him say, 'Dost thou believe in Christ Jesus, the Son of God, Who was born of the Holy Spirit, Who was crucified under Pontius Pilate and died, and rose again on the third day living from the dead, and ascended into heaven, and sat down on the right hand of the Father and will come to judge the living and the dead?' And when he says, 'I believe' let him baptise him a second time. And again let him say 'Dost thou believe in the Holy Spirit, in the holy Church and the Resurrection of the flesh?' And he who is being baptised shall say, 'I believe.' And so let him baptise him the third time.

☐ Why do you think that new converts were baptised three times?

> ### Work to do
> **Paul speaks about Christian belief:**
> > *For what I received I passed on to you as of first importance: that Christ died for our sins according to the Scriptures, that he was buried, that he was raised on the third day according to the Scriptures, and that he appeared to Peter, and then to the Twelve.*
> > **(1 Corinthians 15.3–5)**
> **In this passage what aspects of Christian belief does Paul say are important?**

Key words   **heresy:** religious belief or practice which is against the normally accepted faith

New Testament: the second part of the Bible, held to be holy by Christians

8.3 What do Christians believe about the Bible?

Focusing questions

■ **What kinds of books are found in the Old and New Testaments?**
■ **What is the canon and when was it fixed for the Christian Bible?**
■ **What authority does the Bible carry for Christians?**

The Bible is unique among holy books in one respect. It incorporates not only material that is sacred to itself but also books that are sacred to another religion. It contains:

☐ the **Old Testament** (the Jewish Bible), which describes the history of the Jewish nation;
☐ the New Testament, which relates the story of Jesus and the history of the Christian Church and also includes letters written by various Christian leaders. This material was all written within a century of the death of Jesus.

The Old Testament

The Old Testament is a library or collection of 39 books which contains many different kinds of writing, including laws, prophecy, history, poetry and stories. Since most of the early followers of Jesus were Jews they would have been taught to honour and respect the Old Testament. Jesus himself often quoted from it, whilst writers like Peter and Paul made extensive use of the Old Testament to show that the coming of Jesus had long been expected by the Jews and predicted by their prophets.

The New Testament

The collection of books, 27 in all, which Christians call the New Testament also contains many different kinds of writing – recollections, history, letters and prophecy. The earliest known writings included in the New Testament are Paul's letters, or **epistles**. All of them were completed before about 64 CE, the probable date of Paul's death. He mainly concerns himself with explaining the significance of the death and resurrection of Jesus. The same can be said for other writers such as Peter and John, who also wrote letters which are preserved in the New Testament.

Apart from the letters the bulk of the New Testament is made up of four Gospels and a history of the Christian Church after the death of Jesus (the Acts of the Apostles). The Gospels provide us with the only extensive records that we have of the life, teaching, death and resurrection of Jesus of Nazareth. Three of them – Matthew, Mark and Luke – share much of their material and bring a common perspective to bear on Jesus. For this reason they are called the **Synoptic Gospels**. The first of these Gospels, Mark's, saw the light of day some forty years after Jesus had died. The other Gospel, John's, is very different and was the last of the four to be written. Most of the information in John's Gospel is not found in any of the other three.

The authority of the Bible

A collection of books which carries particular authority is called a **canon**. It was not until 397 CE that the canon of the Bible was finally established to everyone's satisfaction. Yet this did not in itself settle the question of the Bible's authority. This is still a matter of great debate amongst Christians. There are those who will only accept what is in the Bible as the basis for their Christian belief and practice. Other Christians, however, believe that God has also spoken through inspired individuals and the traditions of the Church.

Key question **What is the Bible and what kind of authority does it carry for Christian believers?**

This extract from the Bible is about the Bible:

> *But as for you, continue in what you have learned and have become convinced of, because you know those from whom you learned it, and how from infancy you have known the holy Scriptures, which are able to make you wise for salvation through faith in Christ Jesus. All Scripture is God-breathed and is useful for teaching, rebuking, correcting and training in righteousness.*
> **(2 Timothy 3.14–16)**

☐ Make a list of the different claims that are made for the Holy Scriptures in this passage.

☐ What do you think is meant by the phrase 'All Scripture is God-breathed'?

Work to do

This photograph shows one way in which the Bible still plays an important part in the lives of many people today.

(a) What is happening in the photograph?

(b) Why do you think that the Bible is being used in this way?

(c) Can you think of *two* other ways in which the Bible is still widely used today?

Key words **canon:** a list of books recognised as authoritative by a religious community

epistles: letters contained in the New Testament – most them written by Paul

Old Testament: the first half of the Bible, it differs very little from the Jewish Bible

Synoptic Gospels: the first three books of the New Testament, they take a similar, or synoptic, view of the life of Jesus

8.4 What do Christians believe about suffering?

Focusing questions

- What questions does the existence of suffering in the world pose?
- Why might suffering cause a person to lose their faith in God?
- What have the Christian responses been to the existence of suffering?

As we all know from watching television, from reading the newspapers and from personal experience everyone suffers in some way at some time. To the person who believes strongly, as the Christian does, in a personal God who loves and cares for His children this is one of the most awkward facts of life. It is much easier to ask the questions that follow than it is to find satisfactory answers.

- ☐ Why is there so much suffering in the world?
- ☐ Why do some people suffer much more than others?
- ☐ Why do innocent people, especially children, often seem to suffer much more than those who appear to deserve it?
- ☐ If God is all-powerful, as Christians say, why doesn't He intervene to stop evil and suffering?
- ☐ If God is all-loving, as Christianity teaches, surely He must be moved by the suffering of millions of people?
- ☐ Who should held to blame for most of the suffering in the world – God or man?

People have asked questions like these for centuries and they still remain unanswered. Some, in the face of intolerable suffering, have found their faith in God destroyed. One such person is the famous novelist Elie Wiesel, who was imprisoned as a child in one of the Nazi concentration camps. This experience destroyed his faith in God overnight.

The Christian response to suffering

The experience of suffering is as difficult for the Christian to understand as it is for anyone else. These are some of the things a Christian might say about suffering:

- ☐ God cannot be blamed for the suffering that the human race brings on itself.
- ☐ There is enough food to go round. It needs to be shared out equally.
- ☐ Wars, which kill and maim millions, are rarely necessary and are usually brought about by selfishness and greed.
- ☐ It is members of the human race who are polluting this planet and building up huge problems for future generations.
- ☐ Jesus accepted undeserved suffering and death. This should act as an example to Christians who are in similar circumstances.
- ☐ All members of the human race have the freedom to make their own decisions. This means that they must be free to make the wrong as well as the right choices. Often, it is when the wrong choice is made that suffering results.
- ☐ People grow through suffering. Some of the most remarkable people have been those who have suffered much. When people are under threat it often brings out the deepest qualities of courage and selflessness.
- ☐ The Church itself may work against suffering through those who are thought to have the 'gift of healing'. In the Roman Catholic Church there is the

sacrament of 'anointing the sick' with oil.

☐ After death those who suffered in this life will find that all suffering, death and inhumanity has been abolished. This feeling is expressed in many of the old Negro spirituals, where the slaves looked forward to the time when they would at last be freed.

Key question   **What challenges might suffering present to the Christian faith and how might a Christian meet them?**

The following is an extract from Elie Wiesel's book *Night*:

Never shall I forget that nocturnal silence which deprived me, for all eternity, of the desire to live. Never shall I forget those moments which murdered my God and my soul and turned my dreams to dust.

☐ Why do you think that many people who went through similar experiences as Wiesel emerged with their faith intact or even strengthened whilst others found that such experiences destroyed their faith?

Work to do

1. Compile your own folder of examples, from the mass media, of suffering in today's world.
 (a) Look through them carefully and see whether each of them presents a challenge to Christian faith.
 (b) From your research which kinds of suffering seem to challenge Christian faith most acutely?

2. This photograph shows examples of suffering in the modern world. What questions do you think a Christian might want to ask God after seeing photographs like this?

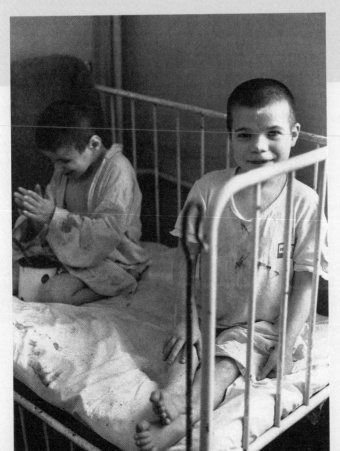

Children in a psychiatric institution in Romania, 1990.

9. CHRISTIAN WORSHIP

9.1 What is Christian worship?

Focusing questions
- **What are the three elements in all genuine religious worship?**
- **How is Christian worship different in Roman Catholic and Anglican Churches on the one hand and Nonconformist Churches on the other?**
- **What is distinctive about Charismatic worship?**

Three elements are expressed in all acts of true Christian worship:

☐ God must always remain a mystery. This will evoke a feeling of **awe** in the religious worshipper.
☐ In every act of worship the worshipper must be aware of the transcendence, power and other-worldliness of God.
☐ As frightening as people find God, they discover, through worship, that they are being mysteriously drawn towards Him.

The hymns that the congregation sings, the readings that are taken from the Bible, the prayers that are said and the sermon delivered by the priest or **minister** are all intended to evoke these feelings. Yet, within these boundaries, many different kinds and styles of worship have developed within the Christian community.

Different kinds of Christian worship

Some Christian Churches – most notably the Roman Catholic, Anglican and Orthodox Churches – have their pattern of worship clearly set out in a prayer book. Each Church's distinctive pattern is called a 'liturgy' and each emphasises formality, ritual and the sacraments. Liturgies also include a number of symbolic elements, many of which can be clearly seen in the central Christian service of the Eucharist (see 6.1).

Many Churches, however – the Nonconformists, for instance – avoid using a set pattern of worship. The emphasis in their services is on the guidance of the Holy Spirit, with a greater degree of importance being attached to singing, prayers, reading the Bible and the sermon. Although most Nonconformists Churches do practise baptism and Holy Communion they place their emphasis upon the written and spoken word. Often art, poetry, dance and other creative means are used to celebrate and propagate the Christian message.

There are, of course, Christian groups that do not quite fit into either of these two patterns.

Charismatic Christians believe that the Holy Spirit can take a person and give them the gift to:

☐ prophesy to a congregation;
☐ speak or pray in an unknown language (**speaking in tongues**);
☐ interpret the unknown language;
☐ heal people who are sick.

Charismatics are found in all the major Churches but they are particularly associated with the **Pentecostal movement**.

The Housechurch movement is made up of people who have become dissatisfied with existing Churches and have formed small fellowship groups which often meet in each other's houses. As they study the Bible, sing hymns, pray and break bread together they consider that they are going back to the pattern of worship found in the New Testament.

The Society of Friends (Quakers) spend time in reflective silence which is only broken if someone feels compelled to speak by the Holy Spirit.

Key question **What are the essential elements in Christian worship?**

The Early Church

They devoted themselves to the apostles' teaching and to the fellowship, to the breaking of bread and to prayer. Everyone was filled with awe, and many wonders and miraculous signs were done by the apostles.
(Acts 2.42,43)

☐ What four activities were carried out by the early Christians and how do these correspond to Christian worship today?

> **Work to do**
> 1. You have been asked to devise your own act of worship. What ingredients would you want to include, and why? Does any particular style of Christian worship appeal to you more than any other? Give reasons for your answer.
>
> 2. Choose a style of worship that appeals to you and attend a service conducted in that style. After the service write up your own description of the service, saying what you particularly liked or disliked about it.

Key words **awe:** the feeling that a person experiences when they are in the presence of a supernatural power

Charismatic Christians: found in all denominations, they place a great emphasis upon healing, speaking in tongues, prophecy, etc.

minister: the Nonconformist equivalent of a priest, his work places less emphasis upon the sacraments

Pentecostal movement: a Protestant denomination which emphasises 'the baptism of the Holy Spirit' similar to that experienced by the Apostles on the day of Pentecost

speaking in tongues: a phenomenon associated with Charismatic Christians which involves a person praying in an 'unknown' tongue

9.2 The Eucharist

Focusing questions

- How do different Christian groups refer to the Eucharist and what do its various names signify?
- What is transubstantiation?
- Which two elements form the basis of the Eucharist and what do they symbolise?

The Last Supper

There are several records in the New Testament of the last meal that Jesus shared with his disciples. The ceremony through which Christians recall this meal, the way that they understand it and the name that they give it vary from denomination to denomination.

The Eucharist (see 6.1) simply means 'thanksgiving' since at the ceremony Christians 'give thanks' for the bread and wine. Through this gift they understand more about the death of Jesus.

The Holy Communion involves sharing or 'communion' among Christians. It is holy since it is Christ himself who brings together all those who believe in him.

The Liturgy (see 7.2) is the title preferred by those Christians in the Eastern Orthodox Church. The word itself means 'an act of public service' and the service itself is rendered to God. Through performing the Liturgy the worshippers are honouring God for his great gift of Jesus. During the service the bread is dipped into the wine and a long spoon is used to place it on the lips of each person.

The Lord's Supper is when Christians come together to eat bread and drink wine in memory of Jesus, just as they are told to do in the New Testament.

The breaking of bread is the title used by those Christians who wish to keep as close as possible to the New Testament since they literally break a single loaf of bread and share it with each other.

The Mass (see 7.3) is the title used by Roman Catholics to describe the Eucharist. It comes from the Latin phrase 'missa est', which was spoken at the end of the prayers when worshippers are dismissed into the world.

What is transubstantiation?

At the Last Supper Jesus spoke of the bread as symbolising his broken body and the wine as symbolising the blood which was about to be spilt. All Christians accept this although they differ about its meaning and significance. Roman Catholics and many Anglicans, for example, believe that after the wine and bread at the Mass have been blessed by the priest they mysteriously change into the actual body and blood of Jesus. This belief is known as **transubstantiation**. The bread and the wine still look the same but they become part of Jesus and so the members of the congregation are able to experience him by sharing in his sacrifice.

Most Protestants do not believe that any change takes place in the elements of bread and wine during the service. In Anglican churches people come up to the altar to receive the bread and wine but in Nonconformist churches the bread and wine are often passed from one member of the congregation to another. By doing this they are showing what they understand by Holy Communion – the sharing of food and drink, just as Jesus commanded, as an act of remembrance.

Key question How do different Christians celebrate Holy Communion and why is the service the central act of worship for many Christians?

A Holy Communion prayer

> *. . . Who in the same night that he was betrayed,*
> *took bread and gave you thanks;*
> *he broke it and gave to his disciples,*
> *saying,*
> *Take, eat; this is my body which is given for you,*
> *do this in remembrance of me.*
> *In the same way, after supper*
> *he took the cup and gave you thanks;*
> *he gave it to them, saying,*
> *Drink this, all of you;*
> *this is my blood of the new covenant,*
> *which is shed for you and for many for the forgiveness of sins.*
> *Do this, as often as you drink it,*
> *in remembrance of me.*

☐ Why does Jesus, in this prayer, tell his followers to eat the bread and drink the wine?

Work to do
These photographs show two ways in which Christians recall the last meal Jesus had with his disciples.
   (a) What is happening in each?
   (b) What words would the Christians in these photographs use to describe the service?

Key words **transubstantiation:** belief held by Roman Catholics and some Anglicans that Christ is actually present on the altar in the bread and the wine

91

9.3 Church buildings

- Why have so many beautiful churches and cathedrals been built?
- What forms the focal point in many churches?
- How might modern churches be different from older ones?

Although Christians are free to worship anywhere – in hospitals, schools, prisons, houses or in the open air – through the centuries they have built **cathedrals**, chapels and churches in which to worship God. Roman Catholics and Anglicans, in particular, have used the size, shape, decorations and furnishings of their buildings to express their belief in the greatness and holiness of God. Only the very best materials, craftsmanship and artistic materials have been considered good enough to honour God.

Other Christians, most notably the Nonconformists, have tended to keep their churches and chapels small and very plain. This is because they are seen primarily as places of worship and so their shape, decoration and furnishings are not thought to be very important. Their buildings, and style of worship, show that simplicity is a very important feature in all worship of God.

The traditional church

The most important features in a traditional church are these:

The 'holy table' or altar is the focal point in most Roman Catholic and Anglican churches. In older churches the worshipper, in facing the **altar**, is facing the city of Jerusalem in the east. In more modern churches, however, the altar is often in the middle of the congregation. The altar represents the table where Jesus shared the Last Supper with his disciples. It is the place from which the bread and wine are dispensed during the Eucharist.

Stained-glass windows: in past centuries these were used to tell stories from the Bible or the lives of saints to people who could neither read nor write. Occasionally today new stained-glass windows are created.

The pulpit is the focal point in most Nonconformist churches since the greatest emphasis in the service is placed on the preaching of the Bible. **Pulpits** are also found in Anglican and Roman Catholic churches.

A font and a confessional: the **font** is likely to be near the door of the church (baptism being the means of 'entering' the church). Roman Catholic and many Anglican churches have a **confessional** which is a wooden construction that separates the priest from the person making their confession.

Multi-purpose churches

To many Christians today the church is not simply a place for worship but also a centre which is used for the benefit of the whole community. In new towns, housing estates and other developments the Church (or a number of Churches acting together) often takes the opportunity of building new premises. The various denominations make use of the building on Sundays and festival days leaving it free at other times for a variety of activities – plays, concerts, discussion groups, and mother and toddler groups, for instance. This means, of course, that all of the furniture used for Christian worship needs to be movable and some Christians, especially older ones, can find this disturbing.

*Roman Catholic
Cathedral, Liverpool.*

Work to do

1. Several technical words are used in this section. Explain what each of the following means in *two* sentences:

(a) a cathedral;

(b) the altar;

(c) the pulpit;

(d) the confessional;

(e) the font.

2. What do you think is the significance of this altar being placed in the middle of the people instead of at one end of the church?

Key words   **altar:** kind of table forming the focal point of many churches – the place at which the service of Holy Communion is celebrated

cathedral: a church which contains the throne (cathedra) of the bishop of the diocese and so is the mother church of that diocese

confessional: wooden screen placed between the priest and the person who is confessing sins

font: receptacle, usually made of stone, which is used to hold water for the baptism of a baby

pulpit: elevated stand in a church from which the sermon is delivered

9.4 Aids to prayer and worship

Focusing questions
■ What is a rosary and how is it used as an aid to Christian prayer?
■ What is a crucifix?
■ What are icons and which group of Christians makes extensive use of them?

The majority of Christians do not make use of any aids to prayer. Others, however, in particular members of the Roman Catholic and Orthodox Churches, find them helpful. Three examples of such aids are rosaries, crucifixes and icons.

The rosary

This is a way of meditating on the most important events in the life of Jesus. A rosary is a circle of beads. There are five sets of ten beads, separated by single large beads. A **crucifix**, on a short set of four beads, is attached to the circle of beads.

The person using the rosary says the **Hail Mary** at each ordinary bead and the Lord's Prayer (the Pater Noster) when he or she reaches each large bead. At the end of each set of ten beads the 'Gloria Patri' is said. On working through each set of beads the worshipper thinks of one event or 'mystery' in the life of Jesus or Mary. There are five joyful mysteries, five sorrowful mysteries and five glorious mysteries.

The crucifix

The cross is the most important Christian symbol and is found in almost every place of worship. The crucifix usually has a human figure on the cross to represent the suffering of Jesus, through which Christians believe they are saved. When the crucifix is empty it signifies that Jesus has risen from the dead.

The icon

Orthodox Christians look upon icons (see 7.2) as a most important aid to prayer. The icon is a sacred picture, painted on wood and carrying many symbolic features. Orthodox Christians make use of icons both in private homes and in public places. Not only are there visible symbols on the painting but even the style and the paint used carry important symbolic meaning. The figures on the icons are usually of Christ, Mary and the baby Jesus, or one of the saints.

Key question   Which aids do some Christians use in their prayers and worship?

The Hail Mary

Hail Mary, full of grace,
The Lord is with you.
Blessed are you among women
and blessed is the fruit of your womb, Jesus.
Holy Mary, Mother of God,
Pray for us sinners now
and at the hour of our death. Amen.

☐ Can you find out why Catholics often pray to God through Mary?

The Gloria Patri

Glory be to the Father and to the Son and to the Holy Spirit, as it was in the beginning is now and ever shall be, world without end. Amen.

☐ Anglicans use the same words in one of their prayers. Can you find out what that prayer is called?

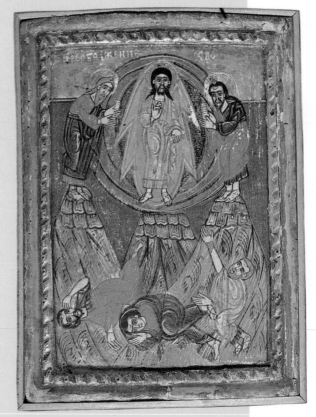

An 18th-century icon from Bulgaria.

Work to do

1. Look at the photograph:
   (a) In which particular branch of the Christian Church would you be likely to see one of these?
   (b) How would you describe this icon?
   (c) What use might a religious worshipper make of an icon?
   (d) What do icons symbolise?

2. Look at the list of the 15 'mysteries' carefully. All but two of the events listed there are to be found in the New Testament. Why do you think they are called 'mysteries' and why have these events been singled out to be remembered whilst using the rosary?

The joyful mysteries
Annunciation of the angel to Mary
Mary's visit to Elizabeth
the nativity of Jesus
the presentation of Jesus in the Temple
the discovery of Jesus in the Temple

The sorrowful mysteries
the agony of Jesus in the garden
   of Gethsemane
the scourging at the pillar
the crowning of Jesus with thorns
the carrying of the cross
the crucifixion of Jesus

The glorious mysteries
the resurrection of Jesus
the ascension of Jesus
the descent of the Holy Spirit on Mary
   and the disciples
the assumption of Mary into heaven
the crowning of Mary as the queen
   of heaven

Key words   **crucifix:** a model of a cross that carries an image of the crucified Christ

Hail Mary: repetition of a set form of words about Mary, said whilst the rosary is being used

9.5 Prayer and meditation

Focusing questions

- ■ Which elements are present in most Christian prayers?
- ■ What is 'the model prayer' and who taught it to his followers?
- ■ What is meditation?
- ■ What is contemplation?

Although public prayer is a feature of Christian worship, most Christians prefer to pray in private. Since God is a personal God it is in private that Christians can best meet Him. Jesus warned his followers against long prayers, whether public or private. Mere words would not impress God.

Private prayer in Portugal.

There are few set prayers which are common to all Christian traditions. Most Christian prayers, however, do contain the following ingredients:

- ☐ the praise and the adoration of God;
- ☐ a regret for sins committed and the seeking of forgiveness;
- ☐ a request that God should intervene on behalf of the person praying, and of others in need;
- ☐ an expression of thanksgiving for the blessings of God as experienced in the life of the person praying.

These different elements all come together in the **Lord's Prayer**.

Times to pray

Christianity is a religion which has no set times for prayer. Many Christians, though, feel that it is appropriate to start the day with a 'quiet time' before they become involved in the business of their day. Many, also, like to look back at the end of the day with thanksgiving and commit to God any problems that have arisen.

Meditation

Meditation is a religious practice that is found in many religions. Many Christians use it regularly as part of their prayer. It is a mixture of vocal and silent prayer. A Christian might, for instance, read a passage from the Bible, try to imagine it and find themselves praying quite naturally as a result. Many Roman Catholics make use of the **rosary** as a means of meditating. In the Orthodox Church icons have been used for centuries as a valuable stimulus to meditation.

Contemplation

This is a silent form of praying which relies upon the promise of Jesus that the Holy Spirit prays within the Christian without any words being necessary. So a kind of loving conversation takes place between God and the Christian believer which words would spoil.

A warning from Jesus about prayer

> *And when you pray, do not be like the hypocrites, for they love to pray standing in the synagogues and on the street corners to be seen by men. I tell you the truth, they have received their reward in full. But when you pray, go into your room, close the door and pray to your Father, who is unseen. Then your Father, who sees what is done in secret, will reward you . . . And when you pray, do not keep on babbling like the pagans, for they think they will be heard because of their many words.*
> **(Matthew 6, 5–7)**

☐ Why did Jesus criticise those who pray in public?

☐ Who does the Father reward?

☐ Why do you think that Jesus warned his followers against using too many words when they prayed?

Work to do

The Lord's Prayer

> *Our Father in heaven,*
> *hallowed be your name,*
> *your kingdom come,*
> *your will be done*
> *on earth as it is in heaven.*
> *Give us today our daily bread.*
> *Forgive us our debts,*
> *as we have forgiven our debtors.*
> *And lead us not into temptation,*
> *but deliver us from the evil one.*
> **(Matthew 6. 9–13)**

Christian prayer traditionally includes praise, regret for sin, petitions for oneself and others, and thanksgiving. How are these elements included in the prayer that Jesus taught his disciples?

Key words   **Lord's Prayer:** the prayer Jesus taught his disciples – also known as the Pater Noster from the Latin form of the first two words 'Our Father'

meditation: a spiritual exercise used in many different religions

rosary: string of 55 beads which helps Roman Catholics meditate on the fifteen mysteries of Christ

10. CHRISTIAN FESTIVALS

10.1 Advent and Christmas

Focusing questions
- ■ **When do many Christians celebrate Advent and why?**
- ■ **What is celebrated by Christians at Christmas?**
- ■ **What does the word 'Epiphany' mean and what is celebrated on this day?**

The Christian year begins with the first Sunday in **Advent**, which is the fourth Sunday before Christmas. For almost 1,400 years many Christians have celebrated this time of preparation for the arrival of Christ. During Advent passages from the Bible read in church services emphasise:

☐ the coming of God's chosen messenger – the Messiah;
☐ the Second Coming of Jesus Christ at the end of time;
☐ the conception and birth of John the Baptist;
☐ the announcement of God's message to Mary by the angel Gabriel.

Christmas

At **Christmas** Christians celebrate a very important part of their faith. Christians believe that God became a man in the person of Jesus Christ, his son. This belief is called the Incarnation (see 6.3). Christians see Jesus as God's greatest gift to mankind, and the celebration of this gift in the Church is an occasion for thanksgiving. Many churches are lavishly decorated for this festival and Midnight Mass, held as Christmas Eve passes into Christmas Day, is usually the best-attended service of the year.

There are, of course, many customs associated with Christmas, although not all of them have religious connections. As Christmas comes in the middle of the European winter, it was used from earliest times as an excuse for feasting and celebrating. The giving of presents was probably an attempt to influence fortunes in the year ahead. The lighting of the yule log, and the decorating of homes with evergreens, including mistletoe and the Christmas tree, also seem to have pagan rather than Christian connections. Even Christmas carols were originally sung for dancing, although Christian words were later added.

Which festival are these Christians celebrating?

Epiphany

The word epiphany means 'to show forth'. The festival of **Epiphany**, celebrated on 6 January, is the occasion on which three 'showings' of Jesus are recalled:

☐ the showing to the Wise Men;
☐ the baptism of Jesus;
☐ the **transfiguration** of Jesus.

Key question   **What is the Incarnation and what link does it have with Christmas?**

Luke's description of the birth of Jesus

> *In those days Caesar Augustus issued a decree that a census should be taken of the entire Roman world. (This was the first census that took place while Quirinius was governor of Syria.) And everyone went to his own town to register.*
>
> *So Joseph also went up from the town of Nazareth in Galilee to Judea, to Bethlehem the town of David, because he belonged to the house and line of David. He went there to register with Mary, who was pledged to be married to him and was expecting a child. While they were there, the time came for the baby to be born, and she gave birth to her firstborn, a son. She wrapped him in cloths and placed him in a manger, because there was no room for them in the inn.*
>
> **(Luke 2. 1–7)**

☐ Why was a census being held at the time?
☐ Why did Joseph and Mary travel to Bethlehem?
☐ Where was Jesus born?

Work to do

1. Read these passages from the Bible:
   Matthew 2.1–12
   Matthew 3.13–17
   Matthew 17.1–10
   (a) Describe what is said to have happened on each occasion.
   (b) Explain carefully what these passages have to do with the Christian festival of Epiphany.

2. Explain, in your own words, the following words:
   (a) Advent; (b) Christmas; (c) Incarnation; (d) Epiphany.

Key words   **Advent:** this marks the beginning of the Christian year

Christmas: means literally 'Christ's Mass'

Epiphany: meaning 'manifestation', this celebrates the showing of Jesus to the first non-Jews, i.e. the wise men

transfiguration: refers to the occasion when the appearance of Jesus was changed in front of three of his disciples – his face 'shone like the sun' and 'his clothes became as white as the light' (Matthew 17.2)

10.2 Holy Week

Focusing questions

- What happened when Jesus entered Jerusalem riding a donkey?
- Which two events in the life of Jesus are remembered on Maundy Thursday?
- Why is Good Friday the most solemn day in the Christian calendar?

Lent is the season of penitence and preparation that precedes the most solemn of all Christian festivals – Easter. Lent lasts for 40 days but in the Orthodox Church it is preceded by four weeks of preparation which is called the 'Great Fast'. Lent begins with **Ash Wednesday**, on which, in many churches, ashes are used to mark crosses on the foreheads of the congregation. These ashes are obtained by burning the palms used on the previous Palm Sunday. The priest applies the ashes, saying: 'Dust thou art and unto dust thou shalt return'.

The ashes indicate that the worshipper's life and death are in God's hands. The worshipper is, therefore, totally dependent on God's grace.

Holy Week

The last week of Lent, called Holy Week, is dedicated to remembering the sufferings and death of Jesus (known as his 'Passion'). On each day of Holy Week up to and including **Good Friday**, readings in church are taken from all four Gospels.

Holy Week begins with Palm Sunday or **Passion Sunday**. It is on this day that Christians recall the triumphal entry of Jesus, on a donkey, into the city of Jerusalem. In many churches, palms are blessed and a procession with palm branches takes place. Often worshippers receive a small palm cross which they retain until the following Ash Wednesday.

Maundy Thursday comes a few days later. The Last Supper was held on the day before Jesus was crucified, so on Maundy Thursday the Eucharist (which commemorates that final meal) is celebrated. Also, on this day, Jesus washed the feet of his disciples to teach them to serve others – this custom is still carried on by some Christians today.

On the day after Maundy Thursday, Good Friday, Christians commemorate the anniversary of the death of Jesus. In many churches it is a day of fasting, abstinence and penance. Vigil services are held in many churches between noon and 3.00 p.m. since this was the time when darkness fell over the land as Jesus came to the end of his life. There are often united Church services, processions and passion plays in which the Easter story is retold.

The day is called 'Good' Friday because Christians believe that through the death of Jesus their sins can be forgiven. Yet, despite this 'good news', the atmosphere of the day itself is solemn. To underline this solemnity churches are stripped of all their decorations and flowers. They remain bare and austere until Easter Sunday.

For centuries hot cross buns were kept specially to be eaten on this day alone. Their origin, as with many Christian customs, was pagan. The bun represented the moon and its four quarters, although the cross was later taken to be a symbol of the death of Jesus.

Holy Saturday

This is the last day of Holy Week and was once known as the 'Great Sabbath'.

This is a day of anticipation for Christians as they prepare for the next day, Easter Day, by cleaning their church and laying out the clean altar-cloth and vessels. At the same time they recall that Jesus spent this day buried in his tomb.

Key question **What do Christians do in Holy Week and how do they prepare themselves for Easter Day?**

Mark described the death of Jesus in this way:

> *It was the third hour '9.00 a.m.' when they crucified him . . . At the sixth hour darkness came over the whole land until the ninth hour . . . With a loud cry, Jesus breathed his last.*
> **(Mark 15.25,33,37)**

☐ How do many Christians remember the hours that Jesus was on the cross?

> ***Work to do***
> **Look carefully at the two photographs. What is happening in each? What particular day was each taken on?**

Key words **Ash Wednesday:** the first day of Lent, during which palm crosses from the previous year are burnt and the 'sign of the cross', from the ash, is placed upon the forehead of each worshipper

Good Friday: the day which commemorates the crucifixion of Jesus

Lent: the period of 40 days stretching from Ash Wednesday to Holy Saturday

Maundy Thursday: the day before Good Friday, commemorating the Last Supper – 'Maundy' derives from Jesus's command (Latin mandatum) to his disciples on that day to love one another

Passion Sunday: the fifth Sunday in Lent – the word 'passion' means 'suffering'

101

10.3 Easter Sunday

Focusing questions

- What do Christians celebrate on Easter Sunday?
- What is distinctive about the worship conducted in Orthodox and Roman Catholic churches on Easter Sunday?
- Why is it important to Christians that Jesus was resurrected from the dead?

Easter Sunday is the most important day in the Christian year. On that day Christians throughout the world celebrate the resurrection of Jesus from the dead. Yet the festival itself has pagan associations. The word 'Easter' derives from the name of the Anglo-Saxon spring goddess, Eostre. The custom of giving eggs on this day not only underlines the theme of 'new life', which is at the heart of this festival, but also the original link of the festival with spring.

Easter Day

Dawn and outdoor services are very common on Easter Day. Both the Orthodox and the Roman Catholic Churches begin their Easter Day celebrations at midnight. In the minutes leading up to midnight each Orthodox church is dark and then, on the stroke of 12.00 a.m. candles and lamps are passed from one member of the congregation to another. Members of the congregation search for the body of Jesus in the empty tomb before the cry goes up: 'Christ is risen.' To which the response is: 'He is risen indeed!'

The main Roman Catholic Easter celebration is the **Easter Vigil**. There are four parts to this service.

- ☐ A new fire is struck to represent the light of Christ and a large **paschal** candle is carried through the church to represent the coming light of Jesus through his return from the dead.
- ☐ Readings from the Old Testament are given.
- ☐ A service of baptism may be held.
- ☐ An Easter Eucharist takes place.

Most Christian denominations, apart from the Salvation Army and the Quakers, have a Eucharist on Easter Day to celebrate the resurrection of Jesus from the dead.

The resurrection of Christ

The four Gospels agree that Jesus was put to death on the Friday and that he came back to life on the Sunday. To the vast majority of Christians this is the single, most important event recorded in the whole New Testament. Although there are some differences in the various Gospel accounts, and Christians may disagree over some of the details, the **resurrection** of Christ does have central importance for every Christian.

- ☐ It stands as a miraculous act of God which shows that the powers of evil do not have the last word.
- ☐ It substantiates the Christian belief that God, through His Spirit, is alive and active in today's world.
- ☐ It encourages Christians to believe that just as Jesus came back from the dead, so they too will be brought back to life on the Day of Judgement.

Why do you think a garden is often used to commemorate Easter?

Key question **Why is Easter Day the most important day in the Christian year?**

Paul speaks about the importance of Christ's resurrection:

> *Christ has indeed been raised from the dead, the first fruits of those who have fallen asleep. For since death came through a man, the resurrection of the dead comes also through a man.*
> **(1 Corinthians 15.20,21)**

☐ What link does Paul see between the resurrection of Jesus and the resurrection of all believers in God?

Work to do
Read Mark's description of the resurrection of Jesus:

> *When the Sabbath was over, Mary Magdalene, Mary the mother of James, and Salome bought spices so that they might go to anoint Jesus' body. Very early on the first day of the week, just after sunrise, they were on their way to the tomb and they asked each other, 'Who will roll the stone away from the entrance of the tomb?'*
>
> *But when they looked up, they saw that the stone, which was very large, had been rolled away. As they entered the tomb, they saw a young man dressed in a white robe sitting on the right side, and they were alarmed.*
>
> *'Don't be alarmed,' he said. 'You are looking for Jesus the Nazarene, who was crucified. He has risen!'* **(Mark 16.1–6)**

Now read the New Testament accounts in Matthew 28; Luke 24; John 20.
(a) Make a list of all the similarities that you can find in three or four of the accounts.
(b) Which details only occur in *one* of the accounts?

Key words **Easter Vigil:** the period during which Roman Catholics 'keep watch' for Jesus to come back from the dead

paschal: word derived from the Hebrew word for 'Passover', it is applied to the candle lit in many churches on Holy Saturday to symbolise the 'resurrection light' of Christ

Resurrection: the central Christian doctrine asserting that Jesus came back from the dead

10.4 Other important festivals

Focusing questions
- What is commemorated on Ascension Day?
- Why is Whit Sunday an important festival?
- Which additional festivals are kept by the Roman Catholic Church?

Although Christmas and Easter are the most important Christian festivals there are several others which are celebrated by the Church.

Ascension Day

Ascension Day is celebrated forty days after Easter and commemorates the return of Jesus to his Father in heaven. Ascension Day falls on a Thursday and, although there are no special customs associated with the day, it is in most Churches celebrated with a special Eucharist. Free Churches (also called Nonconformist Churches), however, rarely celebrate the day.

Pentecost

This festival, also known as **Whit Sunday**, celebrates the birth of the Christian Church. On this day the Apostles received God's spirit and began to witness fearlessly to the resurrection of Jesus from the dead (see 6.4). In celebrating this event on Pentecost the early Christians were adopting the old Jewish festival of Pentecost (see 3.7).

Pentecost is an important Christian festival because it completes the Easter cycle. Christians often use the festival as an opportunity to hold 'Whit walks', which are a public witness to the teaching and faith of the Church.

Trinity Sunday

Trinity Sunday is the day on which Christians reflect and think about the mystery of the Trinity. Many well-known hymns are associated with this festival and traditionally it was the time for ordaining priests and deacons. This is the last universal festival of the Church year to be celebrated in most Churches.

The following additional festivals, however, are celebrated by the Roman Catholic Church.

Corpus Christi

As we saw in 9.3 the Roman Catholic Church believes in the doctrine of transubstantiation and this means that they show respect for the **host** (the bread used at Mass). On the feast of **Corpus Christi** Catholics kneel as a procession carrying the host passes by. By doing this they are honouring the presence of Christ.

Feasts of the Blessed Virgin Mary

Roman Catholics celebrate six separate feast days dedicated to the Virgin Mary.

- ☐ the Nativity of the Blessed Virgin Mary – 8 September;
- ☐ the Immaculate Conception of the Blessed Virgin Mary – 8 December;
- ☐ the Solemnity of Mary, Mother of God – 1 January;
- ☐ the Annunciation of the Lord – 25 March;
- ☐ the Visitation of the Blessed Virgin Mary – 31 May;
- ☐ the Assumption of the Blessed Virgin Mary – 15 August.

The Blessed Virgin Mary was, of course, the mother of Jesus. In the Roman Catholic and Orthodox Churches she is the focus of much devotion as she is thought to stand half-way between God and the human race. The Anglican Church also celebrates some of the festivals dedicated to Mary.

Key question **Apart from Christmas and Easter what other Christian festivals are there and what do they celebrate?**

Jesus ascends into heaven

After he said this, he was taken up before their very eyes, and a cloud hid him from their sight.

They were looking intently up into the sky as he was going, when suddenly two men dressed in white stood beside them. 'Men of Galilee,' they said, 'why do you stand here looking up into the sky? This same Jesus, who has been taken from you into heaven, will come back in the same way you have seen him go into heaven.'

(Acts 1.9–11)

☐ Some Christians do not believe that Jesus literally left the earth in the way that this passage describes. Can you think of another way of understanding these words?

Work to do

1. Describe the importance of *two* of the following:
   (a) Ascension Day;
   (b) Whit Sunday;
   (c) Trinity Sunday.

2. Choose *two* of the following festivals and find out why Catholics keep them:
   (a) the Immaculate Conception of the Blessed Virgin Mary;
   (b) the Assumption of the Blessed Virgin Mary;
   (c) the Solemnity of Mary, Mother of God.

Key words   **Ascension Day:** day upon which the ascent of Christ into heaven is commemorated – sixth Thursday (the 40th day) after Easter

Corpus Christi: Roman Catholic festival on which reverence and devotion is shown to the host

host: name given to the wafer of bread in the Roman Catholic mass

Trinity Sunday: the Sunday after Whitsun, it is set aside to remember the Christian belief in God the Father, God the Son and God the Holy Spirit

Whit Sunday: or Pentecost (see 6.4), derives its name from the old custom of baptising new converts, who were always dressed in white on this day.

11. THE MILESTONES OF LIFE

11.1 The rites of passage

Focusing questions

- What is a 'rite of passage'?
- How many rites of passage are recognised by the Anglican and Catholic Churches?
- Which rite of passage is only recognised by the Baptist Church?

In Christianity, as in all of the major world religions, the most important occasions in the natural progress from birth through to death are marked with special ceremonies. These are called 'rites of passage'. In all, there are five such ceremonies practised by different branches of the Christian Church.

Infant Baptism

In the Roman Catholic Church infant **baptism** (see 11.2) takes place a few days after a baby is born, while in the Church of England children are baptised when they are a few months old. Through baptism a child becomes a member of the Christian Church. The service identifies the responsibilities of parents and god-parents by answering these questions on behalf of the child:

- ☐ Who am I?
- ☐ What is life all about?
- ☐ Why have I been born?

An infant baptism in a Caribbean church.

Confirmation

Confirmation (see 11.3) gives a Christian (of any age) the opportunity to renew the vows that others made for them when they were baptised. In the Roman Catholic Church a child is usually confirmed as a young teenager, and after they have received their first Holy Communion. Other Churches prefer to wait until the child is older. The person confirmed thinks about such questions as:

- ☐ What do I believe?
- ☐ What does God expect of me?
- ☐ What does it mean to be a Christian in today's world?

Adult baptism

Although other Churches do occasionally baptise adults, adult baptism (see 11.4) is mainly a practice associated with the Baptist Church. The Baptists expect a person to be a Christian before they are baptised and the service confronts them with the questions:

- ☐ What does God want me to do with my life?
- ☐ What part can I play in the Christian Church?

Matrimony

Matrimony (see 11.5) is a very important step for anyone to take and the Christian wedding ceremony is intended to make the couple consider these issues:

- ☐ To what extent is our love for each other a mirror of God's love for all people?
- ☐ What can I give to my married life?
- ☐ What do I hope to get out of being married?
- ☐ What responsibilities does being married place upon me?

Funerals

The **funeral service** (see 11.6) that follows the death of a person and precedes the disposal of the body is intended to provide comfort and support to those who are bereaved. It recognises that they will have many questions in their minds:

- ☐ Is there such a thing as eternal life?
- ☐ Can I find comfort and help from those who are still alive?
- ☐ What is life all about?

Key question Why are rites of passage such an important part of the life and worship of the Christian Church?

> ### Work to do
> (a) Why do you think that almost every religion identifies birth, adolescence, marriage and death as being the most important milestones in life?
>
> (b) Is there another milestone in life that you would like to add to this list? If so, what is it, and what kind of ceremony do you think would be most appropriate to celebrate it?
>
> (c) Why do you think that most people, even if they are not church-goers, still make use of the Church to mark these events?

Key words **baptism:** the rite of initiation into the Christian faith

confirmation: the rite of initiation into full membership of the Church, this usually involves the 'laying-on of hands' by the bishop

funeral service: service to accompany the burial or cremation of a person's remains

matrimony: the rite of marriage (recognised by the Roman Catholic Church as one of the seven sacraments)

11.2 Infant baptism

Focusing questions

- What is infant baptism?
- Which denominations in the Church practise infant baptism?
- What is expected of a god-parent?

Roman Catholic and Anglican Churches

Christian parents are usually anxious that their new-born babies should become a part of the Christian 'family'. For this to happen a service of infant baptism is held. Roman Catholics usually have their babies baptised as soon as possible after birth. They believe that baptism is necessary for salvation and it is, therefore, a serious matter for a person to die unbaptised. Anglicans, however, prefer to wait a few months. Nevertheless, both Churches share important features of the service of infant baptism.

The ceremony, conducted by a priest, is held in a church around the font. This font can either be just inside the door of the church, symbolising the fact that such baptism is the door into membership of the Church, or in the middle of the congregation, to show that the Church family is welcoming the baby.

The child must be presented for baptism by both parents and god-parents. God-parents are adults who promise to look after the child's spiritual and moral welfare until he or she grows up. God-parents also agree to take responsibility for the child should anything happen to its parents.

During the service both parents and god-parents express their belief in the main teachings of the Church. Their responsibilities are:

- [ ] to teach the child to fight against evil;
- [ ] to instruct the child in the teachings of Jesus Christ;
- [ ] to bring the child up in the family of God.

From this time onwards the Church is expected to take a close interest in the child's upbringing.

During the service the priest takes the child in his arms, names it and says the words:

> *I baptise you in the name of the Father and of the Son and of the Holy Spirit. Amen.*

Then the baby is sprinkled with water from the font three times as the priest makes the sign of the cross on its forehead. The water is a symbol for the baby's rebirth and cleansing. It shows that by the death and resurrection of Jesus the child has received God's new life.

The Orthodox Church

Although infant baptisms in the Orthodox Church are similar to those in other Churches, they do have some unique features. After blessing the water with a prayer, and breathing on it, the priest anoints the baby with the 'oil of gladness'. The baby is placed in the font facing eastwards (the direction of the rising sun, which symbolises new life) and is immersed in the water three times. The Orthodox Church also carries out the ceremony of **chrismation** immediately after a baptism to complete the introduction of a new member into the Church.

How do Christians celebrate infant baptism and what significance does the service have?

Small children are brought to Jesus

People were bringing little children to Jesus to have him touch them, but the disciples rebuked them. When Jesus saw this, he was indignant. He said to them, 'Let the little children come to me, and do not hinder them, for the kingdom of God belongs to such as these. I tell you the truth, anyone who will not receive the kingdom of God like a little child will never enter it.' And he took the children in his arms, put his hands on them and blessed them.
(Mark 10.13–16)

☐ Why do you think that this passage is often read during the service of infant baptism?

☐ Can you see any similarities between this incident in the life of Jesus and the service of infant baptism?

Work to do

1. Many people now criticise the service of infant baptism and the part that god-parents play in it.

   (a) Do you think that two people should have their baby baptised if they do not go to church themselves?

   (b) Do you think that it is a good idea to have someone, other than parents, to take an interest in a child's moral and religious unbringing?

2. The Anglican Alternative Service Book, published in 1980, has this to say about infant baptism:

   Children who are too young to profess the Christian Faith are baptised on the understanding that they are brought up as Christians within the family of the Church.

   What is the understanding on which children are baptised?

Key words   **chrismation:** the anointing of the body with consecrated oil

This baby is being immersed in water during an Orthodox baptism. What does the water symbolise?

11.3 Confirmation

Focusing questions

- What is confirmation and what is the link between infant baptism and confirmation?
- Who conducts a confirmation service?
- What happens during a confirmation service, and why?

In the Orthodox Church infant baptism, confirmation (and chrismation 11.2) and the first communion all take place at the same time. The Roman Catholic and Anglican Churches, however, prefer to give people who were baptised as babies the opportunity, some years later, to renew their vows and commitment to God through the service of confirmation.

Different practices

There is a certain difference in practice between the Roman Catholic and the Anglican Churches over the time considered most suitable for confirmation.

- ☐ Although provision is made in the Roman Catholic Church to confirm older people it is common practice to carry out confirmation when a child becomes a teenager.
- ☐ The Anglican Church usually confirms older teenagers, although many people who become Christians at a later age are confirmed at that time.

There is a similar service in many Nonconformist Churches although it is not usually called confirmation. The Baptist Church, for example, extends 'the right hand of fellowship' to welcome into Church membership all those who have been recently baptised as adults (see 11.4). In the Methodist Church 'public reception into full membership or confirmation' involves the laying of the minister's hands upon the head of each candidate. This 'laying-on of hands' is the most important characteristic of all confirmation services.

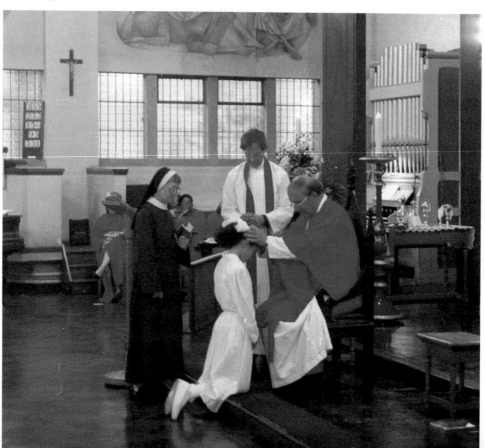

A confirmation service held in a Roman Catholic or an Anglican church is always conducted by a bishop. During the service he asks each candidate three questions about their own spiritual behaviour. The positive answer 'I do' is expected to each question. The bishop then tells them: 'You must now declare before God and his Church that you accept the Christian faith into which you were baptised and in which you live and grow.' Three questions are then asked by the bishop about the personal faith of those waiting to be confirmed, before he lays his hands on the head of each candidate. As he does so he prays: 'Confirm, O Lord, your servant with your Holy Spirit. Defend, O Lord, your servant with your heavenly grace until they come into your heavenly kingdom. Amen.' In the Roman Catholic Church the bishop anoints each person with a special oil (called **chrism**) and says to them: 'Be sealed with the Holy Spirit.'

Many Christians believe that a person receives God's Holy Spirit through the laying-on of the bishop's hands. Others feel that it is an opportunity to 'confirm' the faith they are already committed to.

Key question   **Why is the service of confirmation an important act in many Churches?**

Questions asked during the confirmation service and their responses

Q. *Do you turn to Christ?*
A. *I turn to Christ.*
Q. *Do you repent of your sins?*
A. *I repent of my sins.*
Q. *Do you renounce evil?*
A. *I renounce evil.*
Q. *Do you believe and trust in God the Father who made the world?*
A. *I believe and trust in him.*
Q. *Do you believe and trust in his Son, Jesus Christ, who redeemed mankind?*
A. *I believe and trust in him.*
Q. *Do you believe and trust in his Holy Spirit, who gives life to the people of God?*
A. *I believe and trust in him.*

☐ Why do you think that these two sets of questions are asked of each person waiting to be confirmed?

Work to do

1. In the photograph opposite a bishop is carrying out a confirmation service. Currently in the Church of England most people are confirmed at around the age of 14, while Catholics can be confirmed from the age of 7 onwards. Do you think that these are the right ages for someone to make a commitment to the Christian way of life, of should it come later?

2. Carry out your own survey amongst your classmates to find out how many of them have been confirmed. Write up your findings and discover why those who have been confirmed went through with it.

Key words   **chrism:** the oil used in confirmation by Roman Catholics to signify the idea of kingship, the royal priesthood of Jesus and the inner healing of the spirit

11.4 Adult baptism

Focusing questions
- **What is believer's baptism?**
- **Where are adults baptised?**
- **What is the symbolic importance of the act of baptism?**

Many Christians do not believe that it is appropriate to baptise babies. They see the Church as a fellowship of believers who accept that Jesus Christ has been raised from the dead and lives in them through the Holy Spirit. They confess their belief in this and then are baptised. The most prominent group which believes this is the Baptist Church, which takes very seriously the examples of baptism in the New Testament, arguing that only those adults who asked to be baptised underwent the ceremony. For this reason the act of adult baptism is often called believer's baptism.

What do the three stages of a believer's baptism signify?

Believer's baptism

Many people today want to follow the example of Jesus as closely as possible and so they are baptised in a local river or in the sea. In a Baptist church, though, there is likely to be a pool sunk into the floor at the front of the church and it is in this that baptisms are carried out.

Candidates for baptism usually wear white, as this was the custom in the early Christian Church. Each one of them must be sorry for their sins and have faith that their sins have been forgiven by God. Often they speak publicly, describing how they became Christians. They then descend into the water and are immersed by the minister, as he says the words 'I baptise you in the name of the Father, and of the Son and of the Holy Spirit'.

The symbolism of believer's baptism

Baptism, by itself, does not accomplish anything. It is only an outward and highly symbolic act, indicating a series of spiritual changes which have taken place within the believer:

☐ In going down into the water the person is leaving their old life, with all its sinful ways, behind them. In religious language they are 'dying to sin'. A parallel is drawn between the 'death' of the believer and the death of Jesus on the cross.

☐ By being immersed in the water the person is considered to have made a break with their old life since they are 'buried with Christ'. They recall that Jesus himself spent three days in the tomb after he died.

☐ By coming up out of the water and leaving the pool by different steps from the ones they entered by they are sharing 'the resurrection life of Christ'. Just as Jesus came back from the dead so they have been brought back to enjoy new life.

Key question   **Why do some Christian Churches baptise adults rather than children and how is this act carried out?**

A hymn often sung at adult baptisms

When we walk with the Lord,
In the Light of his Word,
What a glory he sheds on our way.
When we do his good will,
He abides with us still
And with all who will trust and obey.
  Trust and obey,
  For there's no other way,
  To be happy in Jesus,
  But to trust and obey.

☐ In the light of this hymn, and the text, what would you say was the theme of believer's baptism?

Work to do

1. This is Matthew's description of the baptism of Jesus:
   Then Jesus came from Galilee to the Jordan to be baptised by John. But John tried to deter him, saying, 'I need to be baptised by you, and do you come to me?'
   Jesus replied, 'Let it be so now; it is proper for us to do this to fulfil all righteousness.' Then John consented.
   As soon as Jesus was baptised, he went up out of the water.
   (Matthew 3.13–16)
Why do you think that John the Baptist was reluctant to baptise Jesus?
Read Matthew 3.1–17 if you do not know the answer.

2. An early convert to Christianity is baptised with his family:
   Crispus, the synagogue ruler, and his entire household believed in the Lord, and many of the Corinthians who heard him believed and were baptised.
Which came first – the act of believing or the baptism of Crispus and his family?

11.5 Christian marriage

Focusing questions

■ How is an Orthodox wedding different from other Christian marriage ceremonies?
■ What are the three purposes for marriage within the Christian tradition?
■ How does a couple indicate their eternal love for each other in a Christian wedding ceremony?

The Christian Church has always placed a very high value on marriage. The coming together of a man and a woman in marriage is taken as a reflection of that union which exists between Christ and his Church. Although marriage services within the different Christian traditions vary somewhat, they all emphasise that marriage is a life-long commitment and that the two people can expect to be blessed by the gift of children.

Marriage in the Orthodox Church

To members of the Orthodox Church, marriage is a very solemn occasion. They take it to be a sacrament between two members of Christ's body (the Church). The service is full of symbolism to show that it is Christ himself who unites the couple. Not only are promises made and rings exchanged but also, during the ceremony, the priest 'crowns' the couple with wreaths. This means that the couple become the king and queen over their little kingdom of the family, which mirrors the kingdom of God. They are also remembering those martyrs who have borne the same witness to the Christian faith as the couple will bear together. To symbolise their unity they share a glass of wine and join hands as they walk three times around the centre table.

Marriage in the Church of England

In the Church of England **banns** are read on three Sundays preceding a marriage. The wedding service itself starts with the bride approaching the altar, where she is 'handed over' by her father to the groom. The priest explains to the couple that God's original purposes for marriage were:

☐ the procreation of children;
☐ to provide the right situation for sexual intercourse;
☐ to contribute to the couple's mutual help and comfort.

The couple then promise to 'love, comfort, honour and protect each other in sickness and in health as long as 'they' both shall live', before the man places the wedding ring on the third finger of the bride's left hand, saying: 'I give you this ring as a sign of our marriage. With my body I honour you, all that I am I give to you and all that I have I share with you, within the Love of God.' The priest then pronounces them husband and wife: 'That which God has joined together let not man divide.'

Marriage in the Roman Catholic Church

Roman Catholics believe that marriage is a sacrament and so the ceremony takes place as part of the Mass. This makes the promises made during the service 'holy' and so binding on the two people. In the service that follows, it is the couple, and not the priest, who give out the vows to each other. The priest does,

114

however, bless the couple and hopes that they will bring up their children together in great joy.

Key question **What is distinctive about Christian marriage?**

Jesus speaks about the institution of marriage

At the beginning of creation God made them male and female. For this reason a man will leave his father and mother and be united to his wife, and the two will become one flesh. So they are no longer two, but one. Therefore what God has joined together, let man not separate.
(Mark 10.6–9)

☐ What is the main point that Jesus is making?

Work to do

This extract is from the Methodist wedding service order:

According to the teaching of Christ, marriage is the lifelong union in body, mind and spirit, of one man and one woman. It is his will that in marriage the love of man and woman should be fulfilled in the wholeness of their life together, in mutual companionship, helpfulness and care. By the help of God this love grows and deepens with the years. Such marriage is the foundation of true family life, and when blessed with the gift of children, is God's chosen way for the continuance of mankind and the bringing up of children in security and trust.

(a) According to the Methodist wedding service what is marriage?

(b) How does God intend mankind to benefit from marriage?

(c) What is God's chosen way for the continuance of mankind?

Key words   **banns:** the public announcement in a Christian church of a couple's intention to marry.

11.6 Death

Focusing questions
- How do most Protestant Churches carry out burial services and what is the committal?
- What is purgatory and how does this affect the way that Roman Catholics treat death?
- What is distinctive about a funeral conducted in an Orthodox Church?

Whilst the actual form that Christian funerals take differs from denomination to denomination they all honour the body of the person who has died. It is the clear teaching of the Church that the body of each believer will be brought back to life to share in the victory over death that was won by Christ. So, whilst death is a great tragedy, a Christian burial service reminds everyone that death is not the end.

Protestant burial services

Although most Protestant Churches do extend the possibility of a burial service being held in the home of the dead person, it is more likely to be held in a church so that more people can pay their last respects. The brief service is likely to include hymns, prayers, Bible readings and a short sermon. This is then followed by the **committal**, a second service, held at the graveside, in which the body is committed to the earth and to God's mercy. As Christians also allow cremation this final service might be held in a crematorium.

Protestants and Roman Catholics have different attitudes towards praying for the dead. Protestants rarely do so. Roman Catholics, however, believe in **purgatory** and so believe that they have a responsibility to pray for those who have died.

An open coffin in an Orthodox funeral.

Orthodox burials

In an Orthodox burial the open coffin is placed in front of the altar for the service. It is open because all death is a tragedy and a sign of that separation which exists between God and man. The sight of the dead person brings this home to members of the family and congregation. Yet, in the midst of death, there is hope. The Orthodox service stresses the hope of resurrection, with many candles burning and incense around the coffin. The priest wears light garments and vestments. The readings from the Bible stress the resurrection from the dead and the hope shared by all believers in God.

The Christian Church also has special burial services to deal with the most distressing deaths of all – those of children and those of people who have taken their own lives. In the past people who committed suicide were denied a Christian burial but that is now rarely the case.

Key question **Although funeral services differ from denomination to denomination, what essential beliefs do Christians try to express through their burial services?**

This prayer may be used in the burial service of the United Reformed Church:

> *For as much as it hath pleased Almighty God of His great mercy to take unto himself the soul of our dear brother/sister departed, we therefore commit his/her body to the ground: earth to earth, ashes to ashes, dust to dust; in sure and certain hope of resurrection to everlasting life through our Lord Jesus Christ.*

There are many similar prayers used by a wide variety of denominations as part of their funeral services. They all express many ideas about the Christian attitude to life after death.

☐ Who, according to the prayer, decides when it is time for a person to die and how does the prayer tell you this?
☐ Why is the service conducted at the graveside called the committal?
☐ According to this prayer what happens to the body of the dead person and what are the implications of this?
☐ What is the 'sure and certain hope' all Christians look forward to?

Work to do
Read this brief extract from the Apostle's Creed:
  I believe . . . in the Communion of Saints . . . the resurrection of the body and life everlasting.
   (a) What do you think the phrase 'the Communion of Saints' means here?
   (b) What do Christians believe will be brought back to life?

Key words **committal:** the part of the burial service which is held at the graveside – the priest 'commits' the body to the earth and to the safe keeping of God

purgatory: according to Roman Catholic belief, this is the state after death of those who are not yet ready for heaven – in purgatory it is hoped that they can be cleansed of their sins and so made ready for heaven

ISLAM

12. ISLAM – THEN AND NOW

12.1 What is Islam?

■ What do the words Muslim and Islam mean?
■ How many people throughout the world today are Muslims?
■ What do Muslims believe?

The Arabic word Islam means 'submission' or 'obedience'. A Muslim ('one who submits') is a follower of Islam and is one who 'bows the knee to **Allah**'. The will of Allah was revealed to the Prophet **Muhammad** over many years and then recorded in the **Qur'an**. Muslims believe that everything recorded in the Qur'an is the actual word of God and so must be obeyed.

The place of Muhammad

Muslims believe that there have been many **prophets**, including such figures as Abraham, Moses and Jesus, who are very important to Christians and Jews. The last, and the greatest, in this line of prophets, however, was Muhammad.

Where do Muslims live?

Islam began in the 6th century CE in a region where Africa and Asia meet, half-way between the Mediterranean Sea and the Indian Ocean. We now call this area Saudi Arabia. Today, although you will find Muslims in almost every country, the majority of them are still to be found in North Africa, the Middle East and South East Asia.

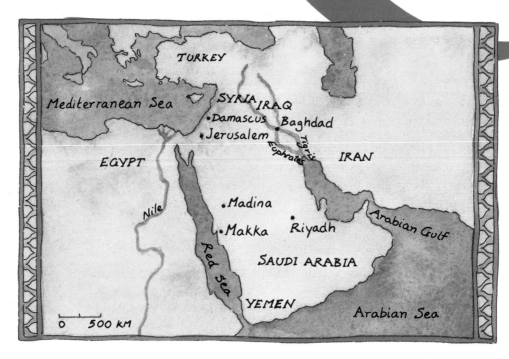

The area where Islam began.

Yet it is something of a surprise to discover that whilst the roots of Islam are still firmly in Arabia, Arabs do, in fact, only make up 17 per cent of the world's Muslim population. A surprisingly large number of Muslims live in Western countries, including some two million in Britain alone. They are part of a world-wide Muslim community, which now numbers about 1,000,000,000 followers. This makes Islam the world's second largest religion, after Christianity, and the fastest growing of any religious faith.

What do Muslims believe?

We will learn much more about this in unit 14. The following, however, are the most important beliefs which bind the Muslim community together:

☐ There is one God and He is the creator of all things. He demands total obedience and worship from all those who would follow Him.

☐ The last of all the prophets was Muhammad, who received messages from Allah through the angel Gabriel. After Muhammad's death these revelations were recorded in the Qur'an by his followers.

☐ There is a Day of Judgement coming when all people will have to answer to Allah. Only those who have faithfully submitted to Islam will enter into paradise.

Key question What is Islam?

> ### Work to do
>
> **1. There are many technical words in this opening chapter on Islam. Many of them have been included in this paragraph. Copy the paragraph into your book and fill in the missing words.**
>
> One of the most powerful religions in the modern world, _____, has about 1,000,000,000 followers. Each of these followers is called a _____, which means someone who _____to the will of _____. _____is the Muslim proper name for God. It was _____ who first received a number of revelations from God, and these revelations can still be read in the holy book of all Muslims, the _____.
>
> **2. Why do the moon and a star make an appropriate symbol for Islam? Remember the early followers lived in the desert areas and had no compass to guide them from place to place.**

The symbol of Islam.

Key words **Allah:** the Muslim proper name for God

Muhammad: (572–632 CE) the final prophet of Allah

prophet: messenger sent by God to give guidance to all men and women

Qur'an: the sacred book of Islam and the final authority on how all men and women should live on earth, believed to be the actual word of God, revealed through Muhammad, written down in parts during his life-time, but put together in a final version after his death

12.2 The Prophet Muhammad – the early years

Focusing questions

■ What do Muslims believe about Muhammad?
■ Where did Muhammad receive his revelations from God and who communicated them to him?
■ What was Muhammad's message to the people of Makka?

There is no God but God [and] Muhammad is His messenger

This verse, known as the **Shahada**, is recited (in Arabic) by Muslims many times every day. This is to show how important Muhammad is. He was not God, as Christians believe Jesus to have been, but he should receive the highest honour since he was the last in the line of God's prophets. As a sign of respect Muslims add the words 'May the peace and blessings of God be upon him' whenever they mention Muhammad's name. But who was Muhammad?

The early life of Muhammad

Muhammad was born in the city of **Makka** in about 570 CE. The city was, at that time, the centre of a prosperous caravan trade between southern Arabia and the Mediterranean. Muhammad never knew his father, who died before he was born. He lost his mother when he was just six years old and his grandfather, who had taken care of him, died two years later. An orphan at an early age, Muhammad was closest to his uncle, Abu Talib, the man who brought him up.

As an adult, Muhammad was first a camel-driver and then a trader. His honesty earned him the name of 'Al-Amin' (the 'trustworthy one'). Soon he was working for Khadija, a rich widow, and, although Muhammad was 15 years younger than she was, the two of them married. During their very successful marriage Khadija bore him four daughters and two sons although the two boys died in their infancy.

The message of God

From his earliest years there seems to have been a deeply religious side to Muhammad. By the time he was 40, he was spending much of his time praying and meditating in the desert around Makka. He was particularly troubled by the religious activities of those in the city who were worshipping many gods. There were 360 idols – of stone, clay and wood – in the **Ka'ba**, the famous shrine which stood in the centre of the city. He was also concerned about:

☐ the rich oppressing the poor;
☐ gambling, drunkenness and violence on a large scale;
☐ women and children being ill-treated.

It was whilst he was meditating in a cave on Mount Hira, in about 610 CE, that Muhammad had a vision. He saw a superhuman being who ordered him to recite a text and called him 'the Messenger of God' (rasul Allah). This text is now part of chapter 96 of the Qur'an.

Taking fright, Muhammad returned home quickly. He was encouraged by his wife, Khadija, and a cousin to understand the vision as having come from God but, after this, for two or three years nothing more happened. The visions then started again. Some of Muhammad's closest friends, including Khadija, began to commit to memory and partially write down the visions. These they regarded as forming the foundation of a new faith. Over the next 23 years Muhammad preached the main message of his faith, that 'There is but one God, Allah.'

He began by preaching to the people of Makka. His message was very direct and only a few people responded to his condemnation of idol-worship. It was only when he left Makka and went to **Madina** that his message was welcomed.

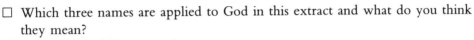

Key question What experience changed the whole course of Muhammad's life and why did he begin to preach to the people of Makka?

The angel Gabriel's message to Muhammad

In the name of God, the Compassionate, the Merciful,
Recite in the Name of your Lord who created,
* created man from clots of blood!*
Recite! Your Lord is the Most Bountiful One,
* who by the pen taught man what he did not know.*

☐ Which three names are applied to God in this extract and what do you think they mean?

☐ What did God do to man?

Work to do

1. The photograph shows Makka as it is today. In this city, before Muhammad received his revelations, the people worshipped the sun, the moon, the stars and stone pillars. Why do you think that the people worshipped such objects and what might they have represented?

The city of Makka today.

2. Why do you think that Muhammad's meditating and praying in the wilderness were an important means of preparing him to become God's prophet? Can you suggest *one* reason why God often seems to speak to individuals in the wilderness or desert?

Key words **Ka'ba:** the shrine which Muhammad purified in Makka and which still forms the centre of worship in that city

Madina: (Medina) the second most sacred city in Islam, the inhabitants of which gave refuge to Muhammad when he fled from Makka in 622 CE

Makka: (Mecca) the birthplace of Muhammad and the most sacred city in Islam

Shahada: Muslim religious verse, the first of the Five Pillars of Islam (see 15.1), which emphasises the Muslim's commitment to believing in the one God, Allah

12.3 The later life of Muhammad the Prophet

Focusing questions
- What was the hijra?
- How did the people of Madina respond to Muhammad's message?
- How did Muhammad conquer Makka?
- What happened after Muhammad's death?

Both before and after the death of his uncle in 621 CE Muhammad and his followers were persecuted by the inhabitants of Makka. Acts of brutal violence were directed against slaves who had become Muslims. The suffering of one such slave, Bilal, who was a convert to Islam, is legendary.

Many Muslims fled from Makka but Muhammad stayed in the city. Eventually, though, in 622 CE he travelled to the city of Madina (see 12.1) in a journey called the **hijra**. This year is now considered to be the first year of the Muslim era. The Islamic year is based on the **lunar year**. Each year, on the first day of the first lunar month, Muslims celebrate the memory of this event.

Muhammad in Madina

To begin with, Muhammad did not find it easy to convert the people of Madina to his teaching. There were many Jews in the city, for example, some of whom were prepared to accept him as a prophet, but who rejected any parts of his teaching that were contrary to their own religious traditions. Gradually, though, Muhammad began to build up in Madina a community of people who were prepared to submit themselves to the will of Allah. As more and more people agreed to follow Muhammad, he eventually became ruler of the city of Madina.

Muhammad returns to Makka

All the time, however, Muhammad was intending to return to Makka. In particular, he wanted to purge the Ka'ba (see 12.2) of all its idols and to set up the worship of Allah at the shrine. He taught his followers to pray facing the Ka'ba, preparing them for the time when they would return to Makka and conquer the city. In the meantime Muhammad taught that it was their holy duty to attack caravans from Makka and any people who stood in the way. A number of battles were fought against the Makkans and a notable victory was achieved at Badr, where 300 Muslims defeated 1,000 men from Makka. This convinced the early Muslims that Allah was on their side.

Then, in March 629, Muhammad entered Makka at the head of a large group of his devoted followers, walked around the Ka'ba seven times and touched the Black Stone (see 15.7) with his staff. He then offered sacrifices and called the people to prayer. In November of the same year, with the aid of 10,000 followers, he conquered Makka. Muhammad entered Makka in triumph as the acknowledged Prophet of God and the city remains the centre of Islam.

Muhammad's death

Muhammad went on his last pilgrimage to Makka in 632 CE. As soon as he returned to Madina, his health gave way and he died on 8 June 632. A day later he was buried in the house in which he had died, which by this time had become the first Islamic **mosque**. Although he did not leave any designated successor, the mantle fell on to the shoulders of **Abu Bakr**, Muhammad's trusted friend. He it was who announced the death of Muhammad to the people with the words:

Those of you who worship Muhammad, know that Muhammad is dead. As for those of you who worship God, God is living and will never die.

He then quoted a verse of the Qur'an:

Muhammad is but a messenger; there have been prophets before him, and they all died. Will you now turn back?

Key question **How did the people of Makka and Madina respond to the message of Muhammad?**

Work to do

1. Read carefully the words Abu Bakr spoke after the death of Muhammad.

   (a) What was he trying to tell the people when he said that Muhammad was dead and that only Allah was alive for evermore?

   (b) What was he pointing out when he emphasised that Muhammad was just a prophet and that other prophets had died before him?

   (c) What do you think he meant by the words 'Will you now turn back'?

2. (a) What was the hijra?

   (b) Why did it take place?

   (c) Why do you think that Muslims consider it to be such an important event?

Key words **Abu Bakr:** believed to have been one of the first converts to Islam, he spent the two years after the death of the Prophet trying to hold together the many groups within Islam

hijra: (the migration) the flight from Makka to Madina of Muhammad and his followers in 622

lunar year: year used in Islamic calendar, as laid down by the Qur'an, it is approximately 11 days shorter than the Western (solar) year

mosque: literally 'a place of prostration', it is a Muslim building for public worship

12.4 The spread of Islam

Focusing questions

- What happened to Islam after the death of Muhammad?
- How far had the Muslim Empire spread by the end of the 16th century?
- What is jihad?

After the death of Muhammad, in 632 CE, Abu Bakr became **caliph**. By that time most of Arabia had been converted to Islam. The dream of Muhammad was one of winning the whole world for Allah and certainly, within a century of his death, a huge area had been brought under Muslim control. Muhammad's followers had carried the message of the Prophet into Syria, Iraq and to Jerusalem and then further west into Egypt and North Africa.

In 711 CE the Muslims took Spain and Gibraltar. From there they invaded southern France and in 732 progressed as far as Poitiers, less than 200 miles from present-day Paris. There, however, the armies of Islam were defeated by Charles Martel (leader of the Franks, who inhabited the north of France) and forced to retreat. Although Christian Europe was largely unaffected by this advance, the influence of Islam in Spain remained for centuries. By the 10th century the three main centres of Muslim civilisation were Baghdad, Cairo and Cordoba (in Spain). Baghdad, the centre of the Abbasid Empire, in particular became a place where Islamic science, literature and art flourished.

The Crusades

When the Muslims invaded Palestine they were attempting to take a country that was holy not only to Muslims but also to Christians and Jews. Christians, especially, struck back and during the Middle Ages this led to the Crusades (see 1.5). The fiercest of all the battles between Muslims and Christians were fought around the holy city of Jerusalem. The most important Muslim shrine in the city is the Dome of the Rock, a mosque built on the site of the ancient Jewish Temple. Its position was seen as a symbol of Islam's triumph over both Judaism and Christianity. The site is also said to be the place where Abraham was prepared to sacrifice his son, Ishmael.

The Muslim Empires at the end of the 16th century.

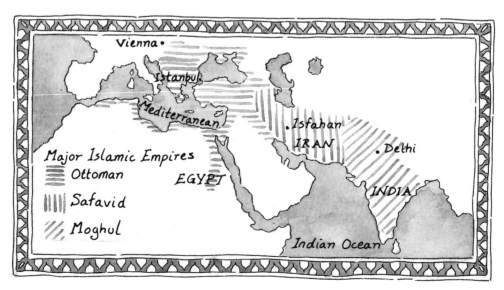

124

The message continues to spread

Before long the message of Muhammad was taken south to Nigeria and the Sudan and by the 13th century had reached China and South East Asia. The message was often spread by merchants and travellers in the course of their business. Constantinople, the great Christian centre, resisted Islam for some time but fell to the Muslims in 1453 and was renamed Istanbul.

By the 17th century much of the known world was made up of wealthy and powerful Muslim Empires – the Ottoman in Turkey, the Safavids in Iran and the Moghuls in India. The last two were comparatively short-lived, but the Ottoman Empire, which was at the height of its power before 1600 CE, did not finally come to an end until the First World War (1914–18).

The jihad

There were occasions when Islam conquered by force. The Prophet Muhammad had taught his followers that a holy war (a **jihad**) was acceptable as long as two strict conditions were met:

☐ A holy war should only be a defensive measure when a country had already been attacked.
☐ A holy war had to be fought in Allah's name to extend Islam and its influence.

Today many Muslims prefer to use the term 'jihad' to apply to an inward struggle against human passions or to an outward struggle against injustice.

Key question How did the Muslim Empire grow after the death of Muhammad?

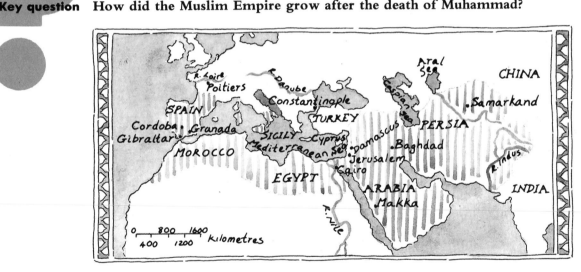

The extent of Islam 100 years after Muhammad's death.

> ### Work to do
> **Use this map to help you name some of the countries which were under Islamic domination by the end of the 9th century.**

Key words **caliphs:** successors to Muhammad, they were responsible for ensuring that the people lived according to the Qur'an

jihad: literally 'striving', in the past it frequently meant a war to conquer and convert non-believers. Nowadays it more often means a struggle against strong emotions or against injustice

125

12.5 Sunni and Shi'ite Muslims

Focusing questions
- What is distinctive about the Sunni Muslims?
- What is distinctive about the Shi'ite Muslims?
- When did the Sunni and the Shi'ite Muslims split from each other?

Within the worldwide community of Muslims there are two main groups – the Sunni and the Shi'ite Muslims. These two groups have been separate for centuries although, on matters of belief and religious practice, there is little disagreement between them. In fact, there is only one important difference. To understand that we have to go back to the early days of Islam.

The four 'Rightly-guided Caliphs'

Between 632 CE and 661 CE four caliphs led the Muslim community:

- ☐ Abu Bakr (632–34);
- ☐ 'Umar Ibn-al-Khattab (634–44);
- ☐ 'Uthman Ibn-Affan (644–56);
- ☐ 'Ali Ibn-Abi Talib (656–61).

The last of the four caliphs was Muhammad's cousin and son-in-law (married to the Prophet's daughter, Fatima). 'Ali was a weak caliph and soon came to blows with Mu'awiya, the governor of Syria and cousin of 'Uthman, who demanded that the assassins of 'Uthman should be punished. In 661 'Ali met the same fate as the two previous caliphs when he was assassinated. When 'Ali's second son, Husayn, tried to regain power he was killed in battle. Mu'awiya declared himself Caliph after 'Ali. Both he and 'Uthman were members of the Umayyad clan.

The Sunni Muslims

These Muslims, who form 90 per cent of the present Muslim population, are the people of the tradition which supported Mu'awiya and the caliphs who succeeded him. Leadership of the Muslim community, they claim, should stay with the tribe from which Muhammad himself came – the Quraysh. They believe that after the first four 'Rightly-guided Caliphs' (Rashidun) the caliphate rightly passed to the Umayyad and Abbasid dynasties, which were both members of the Quraysh tribe. It was then handed down through the Ottoman leaders until the demise of the Ottoman Empire after the Frist World War.

Sunnis teach that all guidance from Allah can only come from the Qur'an and the **Hadith**, which together form the basis of the **Shari'a**. In this way all guidance comes from God and not from men. An **imam** is simply the person who teaches the faithful about the Qur'an and leads them through their prayers. He is not, in any sense of the word, a 'holy man' or a channel of God's revelation.

The name of the Sunni Muslims is derived from the Arabic 'Sunnat' meaning 'tradition'. They believe that they hold to orthodox, traditional Islam as it was taught by Muhammad.

The Shi'ite Muslims

These people believe that the leadership of the Muslim community should have remained with the descendants of 'Ali and indeed their name means 'the party of

'Ali'. They claim that Allah guided Muhammad to appoint 'Ali and that the first three caliphs were usurpers. Some even curse them in their Friday prayers, adding the words "Ali is the friend of Allah' to the Shahada. Each year the anniversary of the death of Husayn, 'Ali's son and successor, is a day of mourning and a time for pronouncing vengeance on his murderers.

Shi'ites believe that the imams were 'Ali's true successors and they should be venerated as caliphs. Yet the order of imams is now finished and the last imam was hidden somewhere by God to be revealed at the end of the world as the **Mahdi**, one who will conquer evil and reward all Shi'ites.

Today most Shi'ite Muslims are to be found in Iran, Iraq, the Yemen, the Lebanon, Afghanistan and India. Their suffering at the hands of the Sunnis over the centuries has led them to stress martyrdom as a means of reaching God.

Key question   **What are the two main subdivisions of Islam and why did they split from each other in the first place?**

Shi'ite Muslims in Beirut.

Work to do

1. **Look carefully at this photograph. It shows Shi'ite Muslims covering themselves in red paint as they celebrate the anniversary of the death of Husayn. Carry out some research of your own to discover:**
    (a) **who Husayn was and why his death should be remembered each year by Shi'ite Muslims;**
    (b) **what the link is between Husayn and the Shi'ite Muslims;**
    (c) **why Shi'ites smear themselves with red paint.**

2. **Make a list of all the differences that you can find between Sunni and Shi'ite Muslims.**

Key words   **Hadith:** a collection of stories and sayings concerning the life and teachings of Muhammad, these form the basis of a large part of the Shari'a

imam: leader of prayers in the mosque; the Prophet's successor, used by Shi'ites for the eleven imams descended from Muhammad, and the twelfth 'hidden' imam (the Mahdi) who will return one day

Mahdi: 'He who is guided in the right path' – the future leader expected by Shi'ite Muslims

Shari'a: all the commandments of God which cover human activities

12.6 Muslims in Britain

Focusing questions

- Where did the first Muslim immigrants to Britain come from, and why?
- When was there a large influx of Muslim immigrants into Britain and where did the majority of them come from?
- What is the probable size of the Muslim community in Britain and where have most of the Muslims settled?

The earliest significant arrival of Muslims in Britain came at the time the British Empire was expanding on the subcontinent of India. Seafarers, recruited along the maritime routes of the Empire, began to settle in British ports. They came from West Africa and India and, after the opening of the Suez Canal in 1869, increasingly from the Yemen.

During the early years of the 20th century these early settlers were followed by students and, in larger numbers, by demobilised members of the armed forces. The rate of immigration was considerably speeded up in the 1950s when many Muslims came to Britain from India and the Turkish part of Cyprus. They were soon followed by others from Pakistan and, a decade later, by Asians from East Africa. The 1970s saw a large increase in the number of Muslims coming from Bangladesh and the Middle East.

The Muslim community

There are Muslim communities to be found in most of the larger cities of Britain and in many of the smaller ones as well. Those Muslims who have come from North Africa tend to be concentrated in London and the South East. Most of those from Pakistan, however, are to be found in areas of Birmingham, Bradford and Manchester.

Most of the original post-war Muslim migrants were young people in search of work. This means that the whole community is still a young one with over 50 per cent of them born in Britain. The children of immigrants from the 1960s and 1970s are now making their way through the educational system, finding careers and starting families themselves.

The first mosques to cater for this community were opened in the 1880s in Woking, in Surrey and Liverpool. An Islamic Cultural Centre was established in London between the two World Wars and during the 1940s it was given a plot of land in Regent's Park by the king in exchange for a plot in Cairo on which an Anglican cathedral was built. During the 1970s a beautiful mosque was opened in Regent's Park and Muslims from many different countries worship there. In fact there are now almost 400 mosques in different parts of Britain – some are purpose-built, while others are converted houses, factories and warehouses.

At the moment most Muslim parents send their children to ordinary schools but the Muslim community is trying to obtain government funding for their own schools so that Muslim children can be taught Arabic and be educated in the Qur'an. A similar privilege is already extended to the Anglican, Roman Catholic and Jewish communities.

How large is the Muslim community?

No one is quite sure just how large the Muslim community in Britain really is. Although figures as high as 2.5 million are sometimes quoted, the true figure seems more likely to be between 1.5 million and 2 million. Seven out of every ten Muslims in Great Britain have their origins on the Indian subcontinent and over 50 per cent of the total are from a Pakistani background. The number of British converts to Islam only amounts to a few thousand.

Key question   **What is the nature and the composition of the Muslim community in Britain?**

Work to do

1. As we have seen, both Christian and Jewish groups in Britain are allowed to set up their own schools with government funding and help. So far this privilege is denied to the Muslim community. Is this fair?

(a) From the point of view of a Christian or a Jew do you think that this is an important privilege? What benefits do you think it might give to both communities?

(b) Can you think of any reason why the government might be reluctant to extend the same privilege to the Muslim community?

(c) Why do you think that Muslims are particularly keen to have their own schools?

(d) How do you think the Muslim community might benefit by having its own schools?

2. Discuss these questions with others in your class.

(a) Why do you think that it is very difficult to assess accurately the number of Muslims living in Britain?

(b) The number of British converts to Islam is very small. Can you suggest any reasons for this?

(c) Can you explain why the Muslim community in Britain is a very young one? What could be some of the future implications of this both for the community and for British society generally?

The mosque in Regent's Park, London.

13. THE SACRED WRITINGS

13.1 The Qur'an

Focusing questions

- Why do all Muslims consider the Qur'an to be a holy book?
- What does the first chapter of the Qur'an say? Why do Muslims repeat it every day?
- What are the main themes of the Qur'an?

The sacred scripture of the Islamic religion is the Qur'an. The Arabic word 'Qur'an' means 'recitation' and the beauty of the Qur'an is only fully experienced when the holy book is read aloud or recited. For this reason, Muslims take every opportunity to listen to the Qur'an being read in public.

The Qur'an and the suras

Muslims treat the Qur'an with the greatest possible respect. This is because the Qur'an is the actual word of God which was transmitted to the Prophet Muhammad by the angel Gabriel from an original that is preserved in heaven. This divine inspiration and authority cover all the words of the Qur'an.

The individual chapters of the Qur'an are called suras and, as they are part of the Qur'an, each one of them is eternal and uncreated by human hands. They are not arranged in the order in which they were revealed to Muhammad. Instead they are generally arranged in the order in which they were collected and written down on the orders of the caliph, 'Uthman (see 12.5). In practice, this means that the longer suras are first and the shorter ones last.

Each sura is identified by a name that is taken from some word or subject in it. The second sura, for instance, is called 'The Cow' since it contains a story about Moses asking his people to sacrifice a cow. The most familiar of the suras, though, is the first, since every Muslim recites this five times a day. You can find out how it starts by looking at the extract opposite.

What is in the Qur'an?

The Qur'an gives guidance to Muslims on all aspects of their faith. It shows them how to live in total submission to Allah and explains how they can prepare themselves for the coming Day of Judgement. To do this, Muslims are given guidance about a whole range of everyday activities:

- the sharing of wealth;
- the treatment of women and orphans;
- marriage and divorce;
- alcohol and gambling, both of which are forbidden completely;
- the lending of money, which is also forbidden, except at low rates of interest.

The Qur'an also contains many references to great prophets and people of the past. It contains stories about Abraham, Jacob, Joseph, Jesus, and Mary, the mother of Jesus.

As the Qur'an is so highly revered, passages from it are learnt by heart and used in prayers each day. At Sunni Friday prayers the imam uses a passage from the Qur'an as the basis for his sermon.

Key question What is the attitude of Muslims towards the Qur'an?

Indonesian boys learning a passage from the Qur'an.

A prayer from the first chapter of the Qur'an

In the Name of Allah, the Compassionate, the Merciful!
Praise be to Allah, the Lord of the worlds, the Compassionate,
  the Merciful, Master of the Day of Judgement.
Thee alone we serve, to Thee alone we cry for help!
Guide us in the straight path,
The path of them that thou hast blessed,
Not of those with whom Thou art angry,
Nor of those who go astray.

☐ Several names and titles are given to God in this extract. Make a list of them.
☐ What does the worshipper ask God to do for him in this extract?

Work to do

1. These three quotations are taken from the Qur'an and they instruct Muslims about how they should treat their holy book:

☐ *He has sent down to you the Book . . .*
☐ *This Qur'an could not have been invented apart from God . . .*
☐ *Behold We have revealed to you an Arabic Qur'an . . .*

What can you discover about the Qur'an from these three quotations?

2. The Prophet Muhammad is reported to have said this about the Qur'an:
  The best of you is he who has learnt the Qur'an and then taught it.
Why do you think that the Prophet placed learning and teaching the Qur'an together?

3. The Qur'an is always reproduced beautifully. Why do you think that Muslims believe that a translation of the Qur'an into a language other than Arabic loses some of the original meaning and is, therefore, no longer the Qur'an?

13.2 The Hadith

Focusing questions
- **What is the difference between the Qur'an and the Hadith and which carries more authority for the Muslim?**
- **What kind of information is found in the Hadith?**
- **How do scholars try to distinguish between true and false traditions in the Hadith?**

The prophetic Hadith and the sacred Hadith

Although the Qur'an occupies a unique place in Islam, a collection of books called the Hadith ('sayings') is also very important. In the Hadith many of Muhammad's stories and sayings are collected under two headings, the prophetic Hadith and the sacred Hadith.

The Prophetic Hadith are the words and sayings of the Prophet himself which show him to be a wise and compassionate figure.

The sacred Hadith are so called because their authority goes back through the Prophet to God Himself. These are further insights that God revealed through Muhammad but which have not been put into the Qur'an. Because of their origins these sayings are treated with the greatest possible reverence.

Sources of the Hadith

Muhammad himself did not write anything down. Instead, a chain of reliable narrators kept hadiths (or sayings) in circulation both orally and also by writing many of them down. However, the number of supposed sayings of Muhammad in circulation was enormous and some way was needed to distinguish between those that were genuine and those that were not. Two genuine collections were made by scholars:

☐ the Bukhari collection, which contains 2762 sayings and traditions;
☐ the Muslim collection, in which some 4,000 sayings and traditions are listed.

To be accepted as genuine, a hadith must include the name of each human link in the chain between the Prophet and the person who eventually wrote the hadith down. Here is an extract from the writings of al-Bukhari in the 9th century, which shows us how this works:

> *Abdallah Ibn-al-Aswad told me: Al-Fadl Ibn-al-Ata told us: Isma'il Ibn-Sayfi told us on the authority of Yahya Ibn-Abdallah Ibn-Sayfi that he heard Abu Ma'bad, the freedman of Ibn-Abbas say, 'I heard Ibn-Abbas say, "When the Prophet, the blessings of Allah be upon him and peace, sent Mu'adh to the Yeman, he said to him . . ."'*

Al-Bukhari's collection of genuine sayings and traditions, with their unbroken chain of transmission, stretching back to Muhammad, were called **Sunna**. In the main, these lay down the way that Orthodox Muslims should behave.

What is the value of the Hadith?

Whilst the sayings in the sacred Hadith are particularly important, they do not carry the same weight of authority as the Qur'an. The Qur'an is the 'eternal record', recorded in heaven and perfectly revealed to Muhammad. The insights contained in the sacred Hadith came directly from God but the form in which they are recorded came from Muhammad. They are, therefore, open to discussion in a way that the words of the Qur'an are not.

Between them the prophetic and the sacred Hadith are likely to cover any question that a Muslim might face. Matters relating to belief and worship are found in the sacred Hadith whilst those concerned with everyday living are answered in the prophetic Hadith.

Key question **What are the two forms of the Hadith and why are these collections so important to Islam?**

A hadith recorded by Abu Dharr:

I came to the prophet and found him asleep in a white dress. I came a second time and found him sleeping. On the third time he was awake. When I sat at his side he said: 'Whoever says there is no god but Allah and dies in this belief will enter paradise.'

I replied: 'Even if he is an adulterer and a thief?'

He said: 'Even if he is an adulterer and a thief.' (The question was asked and answered three times.)

The fourth time Muhammad added: 'Even if Abu Dharr was to turn up his nose.'

☐ What point was the Prophet Muhammad trying to make with his reply?
☐ Do you find it surprising that Muhammad used humour to make a serious point?

Work to do

1. In the text you are given an example of an extract from the Hadith where the chain of those who have passed on the saying is recorded in full.

(a) What test is used by Islamic scholars to determine whether a hadith is genuine or not?

(b) Why do you think that it is thought necessary to record all those who have been responsible for passing on a saying or an incident concerning Muhammad?

2. The Hadith has been described as 'popular Islam'. What do you think is meant by this?

Key words **Sunna:** literally 'custom', the words and deeds of the Prophet Muhammad, followed by Sunni Muslims

A Mauritanian woman reads the Hadith. What does it contain?

14. WHAT DO MUSLIMS BELIEVE?

14.1 What do Muslims believe about God and His angels?

Focusing questions
- What is the foundation of every Muslim's life?
- What is the Tawhid?
- What do Muslims believe about angels?

A basic belief of Islam is that Allah is the only god, and that He is all-embracing. To acknowledge his constant submission to the will of Allah, a Muslim precedes each significant action with the words:

Bismillah ir-rahman ir-rahim.
(In the name of God, the Compassionate, the Merciful.)

These are the key words in a Muslim's life and are repeated many times a day – not only during prayers, but also on rising in the morning and on going to bed at night. They are also recited when any new task is begun, when a person sits down and before any food is eaten.

Prayer beads (misbaha) outside a mosque in Turkey. What are they used for?

The names of God
The Qur'an tells us that Allah has 99 known names or characteristics. It also tells the believer that he or she can call upon God at any time:

The most beautiful names belong to God: so call on him by them.

These names are repeated continually throughout the day. To help Muslims repeat these words without losing their concentration, beads (**misbaha**) are used.

God is One
The essence of Muslim belief is that God is One. This belief is known as **Tawhid**. By this, a Muslim believes that God is beyond all human understanding, beyond time and space, the Truth before all other truths. Nothing

can be compared to Him. Nor is Allah like a human being in any way. He is, quite simply, unique and incomparable.

What, then, does Islam teach about the relationship between God and the world? Allah is the First and the Last, the One and Only Creator. All men and women owe their beginnings and their continued existence to Him. It is by His power and authority that they draw every breath. If that power is withdrawn the person dies. Whilst that person is alive, though, their first duty is to openly declare their belief in the Tawhid.

Angels

Angels occupy a very important place in Islam. They were created in the first place by God and so are His servants – just as we are. The only difference between angels and human beings is that whilst the former obey God perfectly because of the nature that Allah has given them, the same cannot be said of human beings – human beings have free-will and angels do not. Speaking of angels the Qur'an declares:

> *They do not speak before He speaks, and they act by His command.*

The angels are Allah's messengers. Not only do they bring revelations from God to the prophets but they also strengthen what is good in every man and woman. They communicate directly with every believer's soul.

Key question   **What do Muslims believe about God and why do angels play a very important part in Muslim belief?**

The Qur'an speaks about Allah

> *Say: 'He is Allah the One and Only, Allah the Eternal, Absolute. He does not beget, nor is he begotten. And there is none like him.'*

☐ What do you think the phrase 'He does not beget, nor is he begotten' means?

Work to do
1. There is a beautiful Muslim legend which explains why Allah has 99 and not 100 names. According to the legend there is one more name but it is only known to the camel and the camel isn't telling! Behind this legend there is an important point. What do you think it is?

2. Amongst other names, Allah is called the Compassionate, the Merciful, the Forgiver and the Wise.
   (a) See if you can find out some of the rest of Allah's 99 names.
   (b) Are there any names on the list which you find surprising? If so, can you explain why?
   (c) Compare the names on the list with those given to God in *one* other religion with which you are familiar. Is there any title given to Allah which would not be appropriate in the other religion?

Key words   **misbaha:** set of prayer beads. There are 99 beads in all, made up of three sets, with each set having its own distinctive designs

Tawhid: the Oneness of God – a fundamental principle of Islam.

14.2 What do Muslims believe about Satan?

Focusing questions
- Why did Satan rebel against God in the first place?
- What was Satan's punishment for rebelling against God?
- How does Satan still try to lead men and women astray?

Allah has an army of billions of angels – at least one for every human being. They carry out the will and purpose of God and are totally obedient to Him. Indeed there is only one angel who has ever disobeyed God – **Satan** or **Iblis** as he is called in the Qur'an. According to Muslim tradition, Satan was one of the 'jinn' (unseen beings) at the time when Allah created the first man, Adam. After Allah had done this, Satan became jealous of Adam and refused to serve the human race as Allah commanded him to do.

Satan is banished from heaven

After this argument with Allah, Satan was expelled from heaven and he was replaced as archangel by Jibreel. This made Satan very angry and he decided to destroy the human race by leading it away from God into eternal damnation.

How does he attempt to do this? He misleads men and women by whispering lies to them which are designed to lead them to believe that they are equal to Allah. He also encourages them to think that they can hide their sins or thoughts from God. He tempts Muslims into pagan (ungodly) ways and encourages them to depart from the laws laid down in the Qur'an. People who respond to Satan act like a cancer in Islam, destroying the faith of many believers.

Satan can also create the impression that many people are true prophets sent by God, when they are really imposters. Over a long period of time these 'false prophets' have led a large number of people away from the truth.

Can Satan be resisted?

According to both the Qur'an and the Hadith there is only one real protection against Satan. This is for believers to keep Allah and the words of the Qur'an constantly in their minds. The importance of doing this is one reason why the Muslim believers attempt to learn the Qur'an off by heart and pray so frequently. People are only really safe from the wiles of Satan when their minds are fully taken up with the worship of Allah.

Key question   What view of Satan do Muslims hold?

The Qur'an speaks about the angels

And when we said to the angels:
Bow down to Adam;
They bowed down but Satan 'did not'. He was one of the jinn and he
   rebelled against the command of his Lord.
Then God said: What! Would you then take Satan and his offspring for
   friends rather than me, and they are your enemies.

☐ Judging from this extract, why do you think Satan refused to obey God?

Work to do

1. Read these two extracts from the Qur'an:

☐ *The Lord said to the angels – 'When I have finished Man and breathed My Spirit into him, then fall ye down and worship him.' And all the angels bowed down in worship except Iblis, the Devil.*

☐ *'What prevented you from bowing down when I commanded you?' He said, 'I am better than he. You created me from fire and him from clay.'*

(a) Who is Iblis?

(b) What other name in one of these extracts is given to Iblis?

(c) What did Allah command all of his angels to do when he finished creating man?

(d) When challenged about refusing to bow down to man, what answer did Iblis give?

2. Satan is constantly trying to lead Muslims astray. In this extract from the Qur'an the only way of resisting the temptations of Satan is outlined:

> *Those who patiently persevere*
> *and seek God with regular prayers,*
> *and give generously – these*
> *overcome Evil with Good.*

Three ways are given in which Evil can be overcome with Good.

(a) What are they?

(b) Take *one* of them and outline just what a Muslim does to carry out this command from the Qur'an.

3. Islam is not the only religion that believes in Satan, the fallen angel. Describe the beliefs held in *one* other religion about Satan and the influence that he exerts.

Key words **Iblis:** the name used in the Qur'an for Satan

Satan: the angel who, in Judaism and Christianity, as well as in Islam, disobeyed God and who now tries to tempt God's children away from the true path – the Devil

14.3 What do Muslims believe about the prophets?

Focusing questions

- What is the attitude of the Qur'an towards the prophets who are revered by Jews and Christians?
- What was unique about the way that Moses received his prophetic revelation?
- Why is Muhammad unique amongst the prophets and what title indicates this uniqueness?

Muslims accept that the prophets of both Judaism and Christianity were sent by God. The Qur'an refers to 25 such prophets by name, including Abraham, Moses and Jesus, and acknowledges that there have been many more.

This chain of prophets started with Adam, who was both the first man on earth and the first prophet. After receiving a direct revelation from Allah, his descendants soon began to multiply and were scattered over the whole earth. From them, and those who followed in their footsteps, God chose many more prophets and revealed his message to them in order to guide their people. As the Qur'an says:

God chooses for Himself whoever He pleases,
and guides to Himself those who turn to Him.

Abraham (Ibrahim) and Moses (Musa)

Abraham was born in the city of Ur at a time when many different gods were being worshipped by the people there. He rejected all of these gods and saw the unseen presence of Allah behind all things. When confronted by Nimrod, an ancient king who considered himself to be a god, Abraham declared:

I acknowledge the Lord of the Universe exclusively as my Lord and God of worship, and I disown categorically the lordship and godhead of everyone else.

Moses was the only prophet that God spoke to directly rather than through the angel Gabriel. He was also given the tablets of the law on Mount Sinai, on which Muslims consider all religion to be based. Later, Moses led his people through the wilderness to the brink of the Promised Land, guided by the strength of Allah.

Jesus (Isa)

Allah sent Jesus as a prophet to the Israelites when He saw that they had strayed from the teachings of Moses. The Qur'an indicates that Jesus spent three years teaching the people, but it does not say (as Christians believe) that he was crucified. The Hadith says that one of his followers died in his place and that Jesus was taken up bodily into heaven by Allah.

Muhammad

Muhammad, who was born about 600 years after Jesus, was the last of Allah's prophets. Although he was not divine, Muslims believe that Allah revealed his message through Muhammad in a way that was not true of any of the other prophets. This uniqueness is recognised by calling Muhammad 'The Prophet' – a man of God whose life and teachings are to be treated with the greatest possible respect.

Respecting the prophets

Out of respect for the prophets no pictures of them can be shown, whether in mosques, in the Qur'an or in the Hadith, or indeed in textbooks like this. Because Muhammad preached against the worship of idols, Muslim artists are supposed not to paint or sculpt any people or animals. It is for these reasons that Muslims praise Allah by decorating their mosques and houses with the most beautiful geometric patterns.

Geometrical designs in Moroccan houses.

Key question **What is the status given to the prophets of Judaism and Christianity by Muslims? Why is Muhammad considered special?**

The Qur'an speaks about the prophets

> *Say ye: we believe*
> *In God, and the revelation*
> *Given to us, and to Abraham,*
> *Ishmael, Isaac and Jacob,*
> *And the tribes and that given*
> *To [all] prophets from their Lord:*
> *We make no difference*
> *Between one and another of them:*
> *And we bow to God [in Islam].*

- ☐ Which prophets are mentioned by name in this extract?
- ☐ What does the Qur'an say about the relationship between these prophets?
- ☐ What does the Qur'an mean by 'And we bow to God [in Islam]'?

Work to do
What did Abraham say when he was confronted by the king, Nimrod, who regarded himself as divine? Is there a clue in the answer of Abraham to show why Muslims regard him as a particularly important prophet?

14.4 What do Muslims believe about the Day of Judgement?

Focusing questions
- What will be the first thing that will happen on the Day of Judgement?
- How will the fate of each person be announced on the Day of Judgement?
- How does the Qur'an describe heaven and hell?

The Last Day, or the final Day of Judgement, occupies a very important place in the Qur'an and the Hadith. The Qur'an describes the events of that day in very graphic and frightening terms.

A time of judgement

On the Last Day, Muslims believe, the graves will open, the dead will come back to life (resurrection) and each person will be sentenced. The sentence that they receive from Allah will depend on how they have lived on earth. Two terrible angels will question the dead – an event that is dreaded so much by those alive that they recite the Shahada (see 12.2) to those who are dead, in the hope that they will be able to satisfy the inquisition of the angels.

The actions of each person are then weighed in the divine balance. Each person is presented with a book. If that book is placed in the right hand, then the person is counted amongst the blessed. If, however, the book is placed in the left hand the person is counted amongst the damned.

Heaven and hell

The states of heaven (paradise) and hell are described at considerable length in the Qur'an. The righteous will be separated from those who are damned by passing over a narrow bridge (the Assirat Bridge). Only those who have been charitable and humble, those who have been persecuted for God's sake and those who have fought for and in the name of God will enjoy heaven with its beautiful gardens, flowing rivers, lovely maidens, heavenly food and couches to recline on. Yet the ultimate joy for those in heaven is to experience the continual presence of Allah.

The wicked (the damned) will fall off the Assirat Bridge and go down to hell (jahannam). This is the place of everlasting fire and torment. Not only do those who end up in hell suffer physically from the ever-burning fires but they will also experience 'fire in their hearts'. The damnation of Allah is eternal and there will be no respite for the wicked. This is because, after judging all men on that day, Allah will abolish death itself. Men and women will live for ever. What joy that will bring to those in heaven! What torment will be experienced by those in hell!

Key question How does the Qur'an see the coming Day of Judgement and what effect will it have on men and women?

The Qur'an speaks about the Last Day

When the trumpet sounds, the sun shall darken, the stars shall fall, the heavens shall split asunder, the mountains shall turn to dust, the earth shall be crushed, the beasts shall be scattered all over, the seas shall boil, angels shall appear and terror shall strike everywhere . . .

☐ The Day of Judgement is described in frightening terms. What does this tell us about the character of Allah?

Work to do

1. In this extract from the Qur'an the arrival of the righteous in heaven is described:

A provision shall they have of fruits; and honoured shall they be in the gardens of delight, upon couches face to face. A cup shall be borne round among them from a fountain.

(a) What kind of celebration greets the righteous as they enter heaven?

(b) Do you find it surprising that heaven is pictured in such 'human' terms. Is this the kind of picture that you have of heaven?

2. This extract from the Qur'an speaks of hell:

I warn you of the flaming fire. None shall be cast into it but the most wretched, who has called the Truth a lie and turned his back.

(a) The Qur'an portrays hell in very vivid terms. Do you find it difficult to accept that a forgiving God could consign people to hell?

(b) Some people believe that you cannot have heaven without also having hell. What do you think that they mean by this? Do you agree with them?

3. The Qur'an teaches that God is merciful and compassionate, as well as the judge of people. Do you think that these two sides of God's character can be reconciled with each other? If so, how?

15. THE FIVE PILLARS OF ISLAM

15.1 The Shahada

Focusing questions
- What are three basic beliefs of Islam?
- What are the Five Pillars of Islam?
- What do Muslims believe about Allah?

As a religion, Islam is more than a spiritual doctrine. It is a way of life, thought, word and deed. To the Muslim, faith without action is meaningless. Faith motivates action and action brings faith out into the world, where it can grow and strengthen. The faith of Islam is based upon the Five Pillars. These act as a daily guide to every worshipper. They are:

- the Shahada – the declaration of faith that there is one Supreme Being and that Muhammad is His messenger;
- salat – prayers which are said five times every day;
- zakat – the giving of alms or money to the poor;
- saum – fasting during the month of Ramadan;
- the hajj – making the pilgrimage to Makka at least once during a Muslim's lifetime.

The Shahada

The Shahada is the Muslim declaration of faith in Allah. A Muslim performs every act in the name of Allah and declares his belief to anyone who will listen. The Shahada is very brief but it is fundamental to a Muslim's whole way of life. It says:

> *La ilaha ill'Allah, Muhammad rasul Allah.*
> *(There is no god but Allah and Muhammad is His messenger.)*

Faithful Muslims will repeat this statement thousands of times during their lifetime. In particular they will:

- repeat it several times each day in between getting up in the morning and going to bed at night;
- whisper it into the ear of their new-born baby;
- teach it as a matter of urgency to each of their children;
- hope and pray that it will be the last words to cross their lips before they die.

Allah

In the Qur'an God is referred to as 'Allah' and for Muslims this is His proper name (see 14.1 for other names). According to the Qur'an, Allah is the God who was proclaimed by Moses and Jesus, before the coming of Muhammad. Muhammad completed the teaching of all the prophets by offering the final revelation of Allah.

Muhammad was not God. He must not be worshipped. Worship is due to Allah alone, who must also receive the total loyalty of all true Muslims. They must love and fear no one more than God. To express this dedication Muslims say 'Bismillah' ('in the name of God') before any important act and 'Insha Allah' ('God willing') before making any plans for the future. This last phrase indicates the important Muslim belief that people cannot question God's actions but must accept them and be confident that Allah is guiding their pathway through life.

But what exactly do Muslims believe about Allah? Islam teaches that Allah:

☐ is the All-Powerful, Creator and Sustainer of the world;

☐ controls the lives and destinies of all his creatures;

☐ is the Law-Giver, who must be obeyed;

☐ is the Merciful and Forgiving One – whenever a Muslim performs a significant action he does it 'in the name of Allah, the Compassionate, the Merciful';

☐ is the All-Knowing and All-Seeing One, who accompanies His people wherever they go.

Key question **What does the first pillar of Islam establish?**

Light as a symbol of God

God is the light of all worlds;
His light may be compared to a niche
in which there is a lamp;
the lamp is in a glass;
the glass is, as it were,
a glittering star
kindled from a blessed olive tree which is neither of the East nor
the West.
The oil almost glows
even though fire has never touched it:
Light upon Light!

☐ Light is a favourite symbol for God in all religions – especially Islam. What qualities are there in light which a Muslim might want to apply to God?

Work to do

1. Read these words from the Hadith:

   The Messenger of Allah said: 'Islam has been built on five 'Pillars': testifying that there is no God but Allah and that Muhammad is the Messenger of Allah; performing the prayers; paying regular charity; making the pilgrimage to the 'sacred' House; fasting in Ramadan.'

   What are the Five Pillars of Islam?

2. (a) What is the Shahada?

   (b) Name three different occasions on which a Muslim would be likely to recite the Shahada?

   (c) Why do you think that the Muslim belief in Allah comes before the other pillars of faith? What ideas do you think might be associated with the statement 'There is no God but Allah'? How do these ideas compare with the belief in God held by followers of *one* other religion you are familiar with?

15.2 Salat – prayer

Focusing questions
- **What are the regular times for prayer in Islam?**
- **What is the difference between du'a and salat?**
- **What is wudu and why is washing an important ritual before praying?**

After the profession of faith the next most important religious duty for a Muslim is that of prayer. Whilst the Qur'an mentions only three daily prayers, Muslim tradition calls for five: at dawn; at noon; in mid-afternoon; after sunset; just before going to bed at night.

Public and private prayers

Muslims can pray at any time in any place. Whilst ritual prayers (**salat**) are usually said in Arabic, private prayers (**du'a**) can be said in the language of the worshipper. The latter are spontaneous prayers and may include a cry for help or for success in a particular undertaking.

The ritual prayers offered in public are carried out in a disciplined way. Although they can be performed anywhere, many Muslims prefer to pray in a mosque under the direction of the imam. Mosque attendance, however, is only compulsory (for men) for those prayers held at noon on Fridays. Otherwise the prayers can be offered wherever the Muslim is – at home, at work or whilst travelling. They are intended to bring comfort to the person and not to be a burden. Young Muslim children are brought up to observe salat. From the age of 12 they are expected to take the duty on as a Muslim adult.

Ablutions (wudu)

All prayers must be preceded by a cleansing of the person and the place. The ablutions always follow the same, strict pattern:

- ☐ The worshipper must make a declaration of intent to worship God with a pure heart.
- ☐ The hands are washed three times.
- ☐ The mouth is rinsed three times.
- ☐ The nostrils was washed out three times.
- ☐ The face is washed three times.
- ☐ The arms are washed as far as the elbow three times.
- ☐ The top of the head, the ears and the back of the neck are washed.
- ☐ The feet are washed as far as the ankle three times.

Badshahi mosque in Lahore, Pakistan, at Eid ul-Fitr.

There are washing facilities in the courtyards of most mosques. If, however, no water is available, then clean sand will do. When not in a mosque Muslims pray on a prayer mat to be sure that the place itself is clean. Shoes or sandals are removed before the person steps onto the rug. Then, in a state of purity, the worshipper prays facing the direction of Makka (**qibla**). In a mosque this is indicated by a niche (the **mihrab**) in the wall.

Key question   **Which Muslim practices show that prayer is important to the faith?**

Here are two quotations about prayer:

> *Aby Huraira reports that he heard the Prophet say: 'If one of you has a river at his door in which he washes himself five times a day, what do you think? Would it leave any dirt on him?' The Companions said: 'It would not leave any dirt on him [he would be perfectly clean].' The Prophet said: 'This is an example of the five prayers with which Allah blots out all the evils of a man.'*
> **(The Hadith)**

☐ On more than one occasion the Prophet is said to have likened praying to washing in a stream. Why do you think that he chose this particular image for prayer?

> *Allah's Messenger said: 'Prayer said in a congregation is twenty-five times more excellent than prayer said by a single person.'*
> **(The Hadith)**

☐ Can you think of *two* reasons why Muhammad might have suggested that congregational prayers are much more effective than private prayers?

Work to do

1. Explain what this saying of the Prophet Muhammad teaches about prayer:

   Worship Allah as if you see Him; if you do not see Him know that He sees you.

2. Look at these two quotations from the Hadith:
   ☐ *He who abandons prayer demolishes the very pillar of religion.*
   ☐ *If one's prayer is marked perfect, all of his other deeds win the satisfaction of the merciful Lord.*

   What do they tell us about the importance that the Muslim places upon prayer?

Key words   **du'a:** literally 'a call to God', refers to those prayers which a Muslim offers spontaneously in his own language

mihrab: narrow, arched alcove in the wall of the mosque which indicates the direction of Makka to the worshipper

qibla: literally 'direction', refers to the direction of the holy city of Makka

salat: the prayers that a Muslim must say five times a day as one of the Five Pillars of the faith

15.3 The rak'a

■ What is the rak'a?
■ What is the symbolic importance of the various movements and actions in the rak'a sequence?
■ Upon whose example is the rak'a sequence based?

After washing thoroughly Muslims are ready to pray. When doing so they follow a set sequence of standing, bowing and prostration, and each cycle is known as a **rak'a**. Rak'as must be performed at each of the set times for prayer, and the exact number varies between two and four, depending on the time of day.

The rak'a sequence

Muslims begin by making a statement of their intent (niyyah), before performing the following sequence of actions:

☐ They stand up straight, hands by their sides, facing the qibla and, raising their hands to their ears, they say: 'God is great!'

☐ They place their hands just above their stomachs, the right one on top of the left, while the **Fatiha** is recited. This includes the words: 'You alone we worship and you alone we ask for help' and must be included in every rak'a.

☐ The worshipper bows from the hips, keeping the back horizontal, spreading the fingers on the knees, and says: 'Glory be to my Lord, the Great!' These words are said three times.

☐ The worshipper stands up straight and says: 'God listens to those who thank Him' and 'Our Lord, thanks be to you.'

☐ At this point worshippers go down on their knees, bend forward, with their forehead and nose to the ground and say three times: 'Glory to my Lord, the Highest!'

☐ Still sitting on their haunches, with their hands on their knees, worshippers then say the familiar 'God is the greatest' three times.

☐ This is followed by another prostration saying 'God is great!' and reciting three times: 'Glory to my Lord, the Highest!'

A woman performing rak'a. What is its importance?

146

In this way one rak'a is completed. A similar procedure is followed for subsequent rak'as, although the final one is concluded by looking to the right and to the left and saying to one's neighbour: 'Peace be upon you and the mercy of Allah.'

The importance of the rak'a

The words and the movements of the rak'a are modelled on the example set by the Prophet Muhammad. They proclaim in words and symbolise in movement the total submission of the believer before Allah. At the same time they assure the believer that Allah is the Gracious One, who will forgive all those who are faithful to Him.

Key question **What is the rak'a sequence and what are Muslims expressing about God and about themselves each time they perform it?**

The Hadith speaks about prostration during prayer

Allah's Messenger said: 'Make frequent prostrations before Allah, for you will not make one prostration without Him raising you a degree because of it, and removing a sin because of it.'

☐ What is a prostration and what is the name of the prayer sequence in which two prostrations are made?
☐ What effect are the bowings, kneeling and prostration intended to have on the believer?
☐ What are believers saying about God by prostrating themselves?

Work to do
Muhammad himself is believed to have said:
The prayer said in Madina
is worth thousands of others,
except that in Makka, which
is worth a hundred thousand.
But worth more than all this
is the prayer said in the house
where no one sees but God,
and which has no other object
than to draw close to God.
(a) Why are Makka and Madina mentioned as the two places in which prayers are so valuable?
(b) What do you think that the Prophet Muhammad meant when he referred to 'the prayer said in the house'?
(c) What is the sole object of the prayer which is worth more than all other prayers?

Key words **Fatiha:** first chapter, or sura, of the Qur'an, it is a short ascription of praise and prayer and forms part of each of the five daily acts of prayer for a Muslim

rak'a: a prayer cycle including ritual body movements, each rak'a involves two prostrations of the body

15.4 Zakat – giving alms to the poor

Focusing questions

- What is zakat?
- What proportion of their income are Muslims expected to give away in zakat?
- Who has the first call on a person's zakat?

From his early experiences as an orphan Muhammad knew that life could be hard and this knowledge influenced his teaching. He had a deep compassion for all those in need – especially orphans, widows and the sick. The Hadith records Muhammad as saying:

One who manages the affairs of the widow and the needy is like one who exerts himself hard in the way of God.

The meaning of zakat

There is no equivalent word for **zakat** in English. It is often described as a regular giving to charity, alms-giving, a tax or a tithe. It is more than all of these things. It is a spiritual act and the most important duty on a Muslim, apart from praying. At the end of each year all Muslims, men and women, must give at least $2\frac{1}{2}$ per cent of their savings as zakat. There is no upper limit to giving, so long as a person does not endanger the future of their family by giving. All zakat giving should be generous.

The reason for this is that Muslims believe that their wealth has been given to them by Allah. Since that wealth is given to them on trust, it is their responsibility to give it away to those in need. As a hadith reminds them:

He is not a believer who eats his fill while his neighbour remains hungry by his side.

This message is underlined many times in the Qur'an. You can find opposite one passage that reminds all Muslims that it is their responsibility to be generous to the poor.

Zakat is not intended to penalise or tax those who are wealthy. It is a means of 'purifying' the remainder of a person's money and also of keeping their soul pure from an excessive, and unhealthy, love of money. For those who give, zakat is a great means of spiritual blessing. For those who receive, zakat is not charity, but a right that they have as members of the Muslim community.

Who collects the zakat?

In the early days Islamic governments set up special departments to collect the zakat and it was treated just like any other tax. This is still done in countries like Pakistan and Saudi Arabia. In most countries, however, zakat is treated as a personal matter between an individual and Allah. Each person must make their own arrangements to pay the money and decide just how that money will be used. If they fail to do so then it is a matter for their conscience since they know that they will be answerable to Allah on the Day of Judgement. Each person is under a strong obligation to make sure that the needs of their own relatives are met before distributing what remains to others.

Quite apart from zakat, Muslims can also give voluntary donations to charity (**sadaqa**) at any time.

What obligations does the payment of zakat carry for all Muslims?

The Qur'an on giving to the poor

The righteous man is he who believes in Allah and the Last Day . . . who for the love of Allah gives his wealth to his kinsfolk, to the orphans, to the needy, to the wayfarers and to the beggars, and for the redemption of captives.

☐ Traditionally the money given to charity is devoted to meeting the needs of several groups of people in society. Which groups are they?

Work to do

1. A Muslim is taught to 'give something of the means which God has given to you'. What is zakat and how does a Muslim seek to fulfil this command by paying the alms tax?

2. Try to explain this passage from the Qur'an:
Did He not find you [Muhammad] poor and enrich you? Therefore do not wrong the orphan, nor chide away the beggar. But proclaim the goodness of your Lord.
To what extent did the early experiences of Muhammad affect his later teaching?

3. Why do you think that Islam encourages generosity? Do you think that this is a serious and helpful approach to the unequal distribution of wealth throughout the world?

Key words   **sadaqa:** term used in Islam to cover voluntary alms, which show that a person's faith in Allah is true

zakat: annual act of giving a proportion of a person's savings to those in need

Paying zakat at Regent's Park mosque, London.

15.5 Saum – fasting

Focusing questions
- What important event is remembered at Ramadan?
- How are Muslims expected to conduct themselves during this month?
- What are the spiritual benefits of fasting during Ramadan?
- Which groups of people are excepted from the Ramadan fast?

Muslims are encouraged to enjoy the good things of life, including food, since everything that is good comes from God. Yet, for all healthy adult Muslims, one month of the year (**Ramadan**) is a month of **fasting**: they must eat nothing during daylight hours.

Why is Ramadan important?

The festival of Ramadan celebrates the time when Muhammad the Prophet received the first revelation of the Qur'an from the angel Gabriel. This happened on the 27th of Ramadan – the Night of Power. Muhammad himself spoke about the angels coming down and calling blessings on all those who remember Allah, the Great and Glorious. His wife noticed that on that night Muhammad prayed with harder concentration and deeper feelings than at any other time.

What happens during Ramadan?

The obligation to fast during Ramadan is laid upon all adult Muslims except:

- ☐ those who are very old;
- ☐ those who are under the age of 12, although they gradually build up to a full fast by going without a little more food and drink each year;
- ☐ those who are ill;
- ☐ those who are menstruating, pregnant or breastfeeding;
- ☐ those who are travelling.

Apart from the elderly and the young, all other Muslims who miss the fast should make it up as soon as possible.

Each day of Ramadan the fast lasts from sunrise to sunset. As the Qur'an says:

*Eat and drink until you can tell a white thread from a black one
in the light of the coming dawn. Then resume the fast till nightfall.*

The fast forbids the eating of food, the drinking of liquids, as well as smoking and any form of sexual contact.

What is the benefit of the fast?

The fact that Muslims everywhere are taking part in the fast strengthens the feeling of solidarity amongst the Muslim community. The fast also reminds the rich of what it is like to be poor. Hunger is the same for everyone and so the fast of Ramadan makes everyone equal for a short time.

There are also many spiritual benefits to be had from the month of Ramadan. Fasting should be accompanied by prayer, charitable gifts to the poor, contemplation and the complete reading of the Qur'an. By increasing a person's self-discipline, fasting is also believed to draw the Muslim worshipper a little nearer to the angels, who behave perfectly in God's presence.

Work to do

1. In this quotation from the Qur'an Allah is speaking to Muslim believers about the importance of fasting:

Believers, fasting is decreed for you as it was decreed for those before you . . . fast a certain number of days . . . God desires your well-being, not your discomfort. He desires you to render thanks to Him for giving you His guidance.

(a) What is fasting?

(b) Which month is set aside each year for Muslims to fast?

(c) Why is this month so important for all Muslims?

(d) Which groups of people within the Muslim community are not expected to fast?

(e) How are children prepared to take part in future fasts?

(f) What does this extract suggest are the main spiritual benefits gained from keeping the Ramadan fast?

2. (a) Do you know of any other religion, apart from Islam, which encourages people to fast? Find out all that you can about the practice in that particular religion.

(b) Make a list of five spiritual benefits that a religious person might hope to gain from fasting for set periods of time.

Key words **fasting:** denial of the body's natural appetites for a period of time, as a spiritual discipline

Ramadan: the ninth month of the Muslim calendar, it is observed as a month of fasting involving total abstinence from food and drink during the hours of daylight

Outside Regent's Park mosque during Ramadan.

15.6 The hajj 1

■ What is the hajj?
■ What are the spiritual benefits of taking part in the hajj?
■ What is ihram and why is it an important part of the spiritual
  preparations for the hajj?
■ Which groups of people are exempted from making the hajj?

Every healthy Muslim hopes that, by the grace of Allah, he will be able to make
the pilgrimage to Makka (the **hajj**) once during his or her lifetime. It is the
ambition of every Muslim to make this pilgrimage and so fulfil the demand of
the Qur'an. There are certain people, however, who are not expected to carry
out this obligation. These include:

☐ those who are too old;
☐ those who are sick or disabled;
☐ those who cannot afford to make the journey.

An important condition of making the hajj is that pilgrims must leave their
financial affairs in a healthy state and be able to provide for their families whilst
they are away. If they fail to do this, then the pilgrimage has no spiritual benefit.

Why make the hajj?

The journey to Makka, combined with the opportunity to visit places closely
connected with the Prophet Muhammad, add up to a deep spiritual experience.
Pilgrims find that they are purified from their pride and prejudices. Whilst on the
hajj they gain insight into the sort of equality which all people, rich and poor
alike, will know on the Day of Judgement. Along the way each pilgrim
experiences a spirit of companionship and unity with other Muslims which can
be carried over into everyday life once the pilgrimage has ended.

The hajj

Each year, during the 12th month of the Islamic calendar (Dhu-I-Hijja) about
two million pilgrims set out from all corners of the globe to converge on the
Saudi Arabian city of Makka. When they reach the outskirts of the city each
pilgrim must enter the holy state of **ihram**. From then on they dedicate
themselves to worship and prayer. To do this all pilgrims take off their normal
clothing and put on special garments. Men wear two white, unsewn cotton
sheets, one of which is tied around the waist, the other draped over the left
shoulder. Women normally wear a long, plain dress and a head-covering (face
veils are not allowed on the hajj).

From this point onwards all pilgrims are forbidden to:

☐ use any perfume;
☐ have any sexual relations;
☐ cut their hair or nails;
☐ kill any living thing.

Each pilgrim is now in the correct spiritual frame of mind to undertake the hajj.

Key question   **What is the hajj and what are the spiritual benefits for those Muslims who
undertake it?**

Pilgrims by the Ka'ba Makka. What does a pilgrim gain from being with so many other believers?

The Qur'an on pilgrimage

> *Pilgrimage to the House is a duty to Allah for all who can make the journey . . . Behold we gave the site of the 'Sacred' House to Abraham, saying: 'Do not associate anything with Me and sanctify My House for those who circle it or stand up, or bow or prostrate themselves in it . . . And proclaim the Pilgrimage among men. They will come to you on foot and on every kind of camel, lean from journeying through deep and distant mountain highways.'*

☐ Why is pilgrimage to the House of Allah a duty for all Muslim believers?

Work to do

1. Interview a Muslim who has been on the hajj and ask him or her about the experience. Here are some questions that you might like to ask:

(a) Why did you go in the first place?

(b) What particularly impressed you about the journey?

(c) What is the city of Makka really like?

(d) What did you gain spiritually from making the pilgrimage?

2. (a) What is ihram and what change is likely to come over a pilgrim during the time that he or she is in Makka?

(b) Why do you think that all pilgrims, rich and poor, perform the hajj in identical clothes? What spiritual lesson are they intended to learn from this experience?

3. Someone who has undergone a pilgrimage is called a 'hajji'. Many hajjis keep their pilgrimage clothes so that they can wear them when they are buried. Why do you think Muslims associate such a joyful event as the hajj with death?

Key words   **hajj:** pilgrimage to Makka, this is the fifth pillar of Islam

ihram: term used by Muslims to describe the state of ritual purity achieved by pilgrims before they arrive in the holy city of Makka

15.7 The hajj 2

Focusing questions
■ What happens when the pilgrims arrive in Makka?
■ What is the Ka'ba and what tradition lies behind it?
■ What happens at Marwa, Safa, Arafat and Mina?

When the pilgrims arrive on the outskirts of the city of Makka many find themselves speechless. Others weep and are overcome with emotion. Some are simply filled with joy. For all of them their greatest ambition has at last been fulfilled. They repeat over and over again the Talbiya (the Proclamation of Obedience), which was first spoken by the Prophet Muhammad when he visited Makka.

The Ka'ba

As soon as they arrive in Makka all pilgrims make their way to the Ka'ba (see 12.2). They circle the Ka'ba seven times in an anti-clockwise direction, starting from the **Black Stone** (see 12.3), in order to draw closer to their Lord and Cherisher. This means that their first thought on arriving in Makka is of God. (As is their last on departing, as this act is repeated just before they leave the holy city.)

The Qur'an says that the Ka'ba was first built by Abraham and his son, Ishmael, and finally restored again to the worship of the one true God during the lifetime of Muhammad. Since then the Ka'ba has been the focus of Muslim worship and devotion as it lies directly beneath the throne of God in heaven. The Ka'ba has two important features:

☐ the large black cloth which covers the shrine – at the end of each hajj this is cut up into small pieces which are sold to pilgrims as mementos of their visit;
☐ the Black Stone set in the south-east corner of the shrine – according to Muslim tradition this stone was delivered by the archangel Gabriel into the safe keeping of Abraham and Ishmael.

Marwa and Safa

From the Ka'ba the pilgrims proceed to two small hills, Marwa and Safa, between which Hagar, the servant of Abraham, is believed to have dashed frantically in her search for water. To symbolise the soul's frantic search for God each pilgrim dashes between the two hills seven times.

Arafat

A vast camp site is erected by the pilgrims on this plain where Muhammad is believed to have preached his last sermon. As soon as the sun passes its meridian the pilgrims stand, pray and meditate until it is almost sunset.

Mina

The pilgrims spend three days at Mina. On each of the three days they throw seven stones at each of three pillars, which symbolise the Devil. This is to commemorate Abraham's refusal to listen to the Devil when he tried to persuade him not to sacrifice his son. The pilgrims also sacrifice an animal.

The pilgrimage is now over. The pilgrims return to their homes and their local Muslim communities. The hajjis, as the pilgrims are called, are now expected to share the blessings of the pilgrimage with those who could not go.

Key question Why is the hajj the greatest of all spiritual experiences for a Muslim?

What is the significance of the places the pilgrims visit during the hajj?

Work to do

1. Copy this map into your book. Then explain what a Muslim pilgrim does when he reaches each of the following places:

   (a) Makka; (b) Marwa and Safa (in Makka); (c) Arafat; (d) Mina.

2. In this extract from his autobiography the American Black Muslim, Malcolm X, is describing the emotional effect that the pilgrimage to Makka had upon him:

> They were of all colours, from blue-eyed blondes to black-skinned Africans. But we were all participating in the same ritual, displaying a spirit of unity and brotherhood that my experiences in America had led me to believe never could exist between the white and the non-white.

What so impressed Malcolm X about the hajj and how did his experience of the pilgrimage affect him?

Key words **Black Stone:** oval and about 18 cm in diameter, this is thought to be a meteorite and is taken to be a symbol of that which comes down to earth from heaven

155

16. WORSHIP AND FESTIVALS

16.1 The mosque – the house of prayer

Focusing questions

- What features do all purpose-built mosques contain?
- What is the Adhan and who issues it from the minaret of a mosque?
- What happens in mosques every Friday morning?

Muslims pray together in a mosque (the house of prayer). This building is not only the focal point for Muslim worship but also the centre of the whole Muslim community. The building itself, however, is not essential to prayer. Muhammad taught his followers that prayer can be offered to Allah anywhere:

Wherever the hour of prayer overtakes you, you shall perform it.
That place is a mosque.

Yet he also taught them that whoever built a mosque would enter straight into paradise, so pleasing would their act be to God. Although a mosque in Britain is most likely to be a converted house or church, a purpose-built mosque contains the following: a main hall in which the prayers are conducted; facilities for washing; places set aside for study and teaching children; a room for preparing the dead for burial.

The outside of the mosque

Although some of the world's most beautiful buildings are mosques, such as the Dome of the Rock in Jerusalem, most of them are simply rectangular in shape and very plain inside. All mosques have two distinguishing features:

- ☐ a dome – this is onion-shaped and represents the universe over which Allah has control;
- ☐ **minarets** from which the call to prayer (the **Adhan**) is given by the **muezzin** five times each day.

As we saw in 15.2, each Muslim must wash thoroughly before entering the mosque. This requires running water, and taps are placed in an outside courtyard for this purpose.

Inside the mosque

When Muslims enter a mosque to pray, they remove their shoes as a sign of respect to Allah. There are no seats in a mosque. On entering the main hall Muslims spread their prayer mat (see 15.2) on the floor. The decoration on the mat must include an arch, and when the mat is laid down, this arch must face in the direction of Makka. No pictures or statues are allowed inside a mosque, although the walls and pillars can be decorated with patterns or verses from the Qur'an.

The main service in the mosque is Friday prayers when all male Muslims are expected to attend unless they are ill or travelling. At this service the imam leads the congregation through their prayers and delivers a sermon from a raised platform (minbar). In his sermon the imam will explain the relevance of a passage from the Qur'an. Women are not under any obligation to attend the mosque on this day, but those that do attend, pray separately from the men. This is for reasons of modesty, given the nature of the praying positions.

The mosque is also open for prayers and other activities on the other days of the week. Many Muslims prefer to say their daily prayers in the mosque rather than at home or at their workplace. During the day the building is often used as a community centre as well – especially, in Britain, in those areas where there are many Muslims.

Key question   **What are the main features outside and inside a mosque?**

The Adhan

God is most great, God is most great, God is most great, God is most great.
I bear witness that there is no god but Allah.
I bear witness that there is no god but Allah.
I bear witness that Muhammad is the Prophet of Allah.
I bear witness that Muhammad is the Prophet of Allah.
Come to prayer, come to prayer,
Come to success, come to success,
God is most great, God is most great.
There is no god but Allah.

☐ This call to prayer mentions several aspects of Muslim belief. What are they?

A house mosque in Birmingham.

Work to do

1. In this photograph you can see a house being used as a mosque. Sometimes churches are converted into mosques. Suppose that you were on a committee which had to consider a request from a local Muslim community which wanted to buy a church that was no longer used. Would you support selling it to them or not? Give your reasons for your decision.

2. Is there a mosque in your area? If so, see if a visit can be arranged. Decide what questions to ask before you go.

Key words   **Adhan:** call to prayer which goes out at dawn, midday, mid-afternoon, sunset and after the fall of darkness

minaret: the tower of a Muslim mosque from which the muezzin calls the faithful to prayer five times each day

muezzin: the official of the mosque who issues the call to prayer each day

16.2 The festival of Eid ul-Fitr

Focusing questions
- **What important event is commemorated at the festival of Eid ul-Fitr?**
- **What is Zakat ul-Fitr?**
- **How is Eid ul-Fitr celebrated?**

The fast of Ramadan ends with the three-day festival of Eid ul-Fitr. Beginning on the first day of the tenth month of the year – the month of Shawwal – this festival brings the whole Muslim community together for a time of prayer and celebration.

Beginning Eid ul-Fitr

Before Eid ul-Fitr begins, Muslims observe Zakat ul-Fitr. This is the time when individuals give money to help those within their community who are in need. The amount given should be enough for a poor family to buy a meal so that no one need feel deprived during Eid ul-Fitr.

Few people go to bed on the last night of Ramadan. They meet on the streets to watch for the new moon rising. With the new moon a new month has begun and Eid ul-Fitr has started. Early on the first morning the whole family attends a service in the mosque. Sometimes several services need to be held as the mosque is not large enough to hold all those who want to thank Allah that the fast is now over. At this service the imam leads the people in special prayers before delivering a sermon in which the people are reminded that they have a special responsibility towards the poor within the Muslim community. The congregation are told that they should be generous, since this is a way of thanking Allah for His goodness to them. The imam also reminds those present that they have only successfully completed the fast because of Allah's help. They are told that Muhammad himself promised his followers two rewards for fasting:

☐ the pleasure that is given to them by Allah when the fast has been successfully completed;

☐ a reward from Allah on the Day of Judgement.

Celebrating Eid ul-Fitr

After the service everyone goes home ¬ often to large family gatherings and parties. The houses are decorated with Eid greetings cards and these often carry the words 'Eid Mubarak' (Have a happy and blessed festival). Sometimes presents are exchanged and opened, and special cakes and sugary sweets are given to the children. Many families visit the houses of relatives and friends to share a large meal, which includes a sweet pudding containing dates and milk. Ramadan and Eid ul-Fitr act as a reminder to everyone of the time that Muhammad spent in the desert. Ramadan is the time when all Muslims go through the 'desert' together, but now, as they look towards the coming months, they can expect to enjoy Allah's blessings once again.

Finally, a visit is paid to the cemetery. Everyone is anxious to remember those who have been separated from the celebrations by death. The Muslim family is completely united and this includes both the living and the dead.

Key question Which themes are brought together in the festival of Eid ul-Fitr?

In this extract a Muslim is describing how much members of the Muslim community enjoy Eid ul-Fitr:

> You cannot imagine the joy and relief that a person feels after they have fasted for a whole month. They are so thankful to Allah that they have been able to take the strain and complete an obligation of their faith. Did I say obligation? It is not really that. It is something that has been willingly accepted — but that does not mean that a Muslim is not pleased when it is over.

☐ What is the main emotion felt by this Muslim now that Ramadan is over?

Work to do
1. Why do you think that Eid ul-Fitr is such an important festival in the Muslim community? Can you explain why Zakat ul-Fitr is an important part of the festival? What does zakat tell us about the Muslim attitude towards the poor?

2. Presents are exchanged at Eid ul-Fitr. Apart from the obvious pleasure in giving and receiving, do you think that there is a spiritual message behind this particular practice?

Eid greetings cards.

16.3 The festival of Eid ul-Adha

Focusing questions

- What is the link between the festival of Eid ul-Adha and the pilgrimage to Makka?
- Why is an animal sacrificed at this festival and what does its death symbolise?
- What is halal and why is it important that all meat is killed in a certain way?
- What is the spiritual significance of halal?

Eid ul-Adha is the festival which begins on the tenth day of the pilgrimage to Makka and lasts for two or three days. Although it is particularly significant for those on the pilgrimage, Muslims all over the world join in the celebrations. In this way they are experiencing the bond which unites one Muslim with another.

The origin of Eid ul-Adha

Muslims believe that the origins of this festival go right back to the beginning of Islam. Centuries before Muhammad was born there was another prophet called Ibrahim (Abraham) and his story is told in the Qur'an. He was ready to sacrifice his only son, Ishmael, to show that he was willing to obey Allah fully, but at the last moment God provided a way out – a ram caught by his horns in a bush to be sacrificed in his place. Eid ul-Adha symbolises the submission and commitment of each Muslim to the will of Allah.

A Muslim family visiting a halal butcher's in Slough, Berkshire.

Eid ul-Adha – the feast of sacrifices

The sacrifice of an animal forms the centre point of this festival. Each Muslim family must select for sacrifice a perfect animal (a sheep, goat, cow or camel), which, in many cases, the man of the house will slaughter himself. This is the ideal, since it forces that family to face up to the reality of sacrifice. In Western countries, however, such slaughter is not allowed: the animals must be killed by a licensed slaughterer in an abattoir.

Strict religious conditions are laid down in Islam for the slaughter of animals. First the animal is turned to face Makka whilst the slaughterer calls upon the name of Allah. Verses from the Qur'an are then recited as a very sharp knife is drawn across the jugular vein in the neck of the animal. The blood is allowed to drain away. Muslims believe that eating blood is unclean – a belief that is shared by many other faiths, including Judaism. Meat killed in this ritual way is called **halal** meat. Animals killed incorrectly, and so forbidden for Muslims, are called **haram**.

Once the necessary ritual has been carried out, the carcase of the animal is cut up for food. The family that has provided the animal keeps one-third of the carcase for its own needs and distributes the remainder amongst the poor people in the community. Often this is the only time in the year that such people have meat to eat.

Key question   **What lies at the heart of the festival of Eid ul-Adha?**

In this extract a Muslim is describing the importance of the festival of Eid ul-Adha:

> *All of these people who go on the hajj have made considerable sacrifices and this is part of the spiritual message of the pilgrimage. This element of sacrifice is expressed in the festival of Eid ul-Adha. Those who stay at home also want to be reminded of Abraham, who was prepared to sacrifice his son if Allah demanded it. It reminds us that in the cause of God's religion we should all be prepared to sacrifice everything.*

☐ In the modern world, what extreme sacrifice do you think a Muslim might make?

Work to do

1. Read Genesis 22.1–13 in your Bible. Can you find *one* important way in which this story differs from the version in the Qur'an?

2. The Islamic regulations about slaughtering animals conflict with official regulations in this country. Bearing in mind that there is a sizeable Muslim community in this country, do you think that all minority groups should be made to conform to the laws of the country in which they live – even if those laws conflict with their religious rules?

3. Why do you think that many religions teach that the life of an animal, or a human being, is in their blood? Can you find out about one religious faith which bans all blood transfusions for this very reason?

Key words   **halal:** literally 'allowed', term applied to any meat that has been killed in accordance with Muslim law and is therefore fit for Muslims to eat

haram: meat that is not killed according to Muslim regulations and therefore unfit to eat

17. THE MUSLIM FAMILY

17.1 Children

Focusing questions
- **What is the Umma?**
- **What is the aqiqa ceremony?**
- **What is the bismillah ceremony and what does it mark the beginning of?**

What do you think this father is whispering to his new-born baby?

Since all babies born into a Muslim family are received as gifts from Allah, they are welcomed into the Umma – the worldwide family of Islam – soon after birth. Indeed, within a few minutes, the father of the child takes it into his arms and whispers the Adhan (the call to prayer) in its right ear:

> *God is the greatest . . . I bear witness that there is no God but Allah . . . I bear witness that Muhammad is the messenger of Allah . . . Come to prayer . . . Come to success . . . God is the greatest . . . There is no God but Allah.*

This means that the first word that the baby hears is the name of God. After the Adhan is recited, a tiny piece of sugar or date is placed on the baby's tongue by an elderly relative, expressing the hope that the child will grow up to be obedient and kind.

Aqiqa

Seven days after birth the **aqiqa** ceremony takes place, at which several important things happen:

- ☐ The child's head is shaved, to symbolise the removal of all misfortune. Gold and silver of equivalent weight to the shaven hair is then given to the poor. If the baby is a girl one sheep or goat is sacrificed. For a boy two animals are sacrificed. The meat is sweetened as it is cooked, and one-third is given away to relatives and two-thirds to the poor.
- ☐ The child receives its name. In Islam the choice of the name is very important and many names are derived from those of Allah, Muhammad or other great Muslim leaders of the past.
- ☐ In Islam, as in the Jewish faith, most boys are circumcised when they are eight days old, though Muslim tradition does allow parents to carry out the circumcision (known as 'khitan') at any time before the child is ten years old.

The bismillah ceremony

In some parts of the Muslim world the **bismillah** (see 14.1) ceremony takes place when a child is exactly four years, four months and four days old. The ceremony commemorates the first occasion that the angel Gabriel appeared to Muhammad and marks the beginning of the child's religious education. The child learns the first lesson from the Qur'an off by heart:

> *In the name of God, the Compassionate, the Merciful.*

To celebrate the occasion the child receives a gift of sweets.

Religious education

Muslims take the religious education of their children very seriously. This education, which begins at bismillah, continues at the madressa (the 'school' in the mosque), which the child now begins to attend regularly. In this school every child learns to read and recite Arabic so that they can understand the Qur'an in its original language. They will also begin the life-long process of learning many passages from the Holy Book off by heart. Each child also learns how to perform the rak'a (see 15.3).

Key question How do the Muslim ceremonies performed on a young child show that he or she is special in the eyes of God?

The Qur'an on the bestowing of children

> To Allah belongs the kingdoms of the heavens and the earth. He creates what He wills. He bestows sons and daughters according to His will.
> Or he bestows both sons and daughters, and leaves barren whom He chooses, for He is full of knowledge and power.

☐ What point is this extract making about the birth of children?

Work to do

1. At the bismillah some verses are read from the Qur'an to the child, who is made to repeat them:

   Recite! In the name of the Lord who created, created man from a clot of blood. Proclaim: your Lord is most generous, who taught by the pen, taught man what he did not know.

   What happens at the bismillah and why is this reading particularly appropriate?

2. Why do you think that at the aqiqa the sacrifice for a boy is double that for a girl?

3. Do you think that it is a good idea for the children of religious parents to be taught about their faith at the earliest possible time?
   (a) What do you think might be the main advantage of doing this?
   (b) What do you think might be the main disadvantage of doing this?

Key words **aqiqa:** ceremony at which Muslim children receive their names and at which many Muslim boys are circumcised

bismillah: abbreviation of 'bismillah ir-rahman ir-rahim', literally 'in the name of God, the Merciful, the Compassionate' – it comes before every sura in the Qur'an except one (Sura 9)

17.2 Marriage

Focusing questions
- What must a man give a woman under Muslim marriage laws?
- What is polygamy?
- What is an 'arranged marriage' and why do Muslims maintain that this is a beneficial arrangement?

Muslims are encouraged to marry and the Qur'an allows Muslim men to have up to four wives, although he must be able to treat each of them equally. In practice, though, polygamy is only practised by a small number of people. Today it usually only occurs when the first wife is unable to have children or falls seriously ill. There is no provision in Islam for a woman to have more than one husband.

Muslim tradition states that people can only achieve their full potential if they marry and have children. This is felt to be particularly true of women – as one hadith puts it:

Paradise lies at the feet of mothers.

Arranged marriages

Muslims are encouraged to see marriage as a life-long relationship and, for this reason, great emphasis is laid upon ensuring that marriage partners are compatible. In most Muslim families, parents and relatives, as well as the marriage partners, are involved in making this decision. This is called an **arranged marriage**.

When a Muslim man wants to marry a woman he presents himself to her and her family. He makes an enquiry about the conditions for the girl's marriage. If both parties reach an agreement then the engagement is announced and a wedding-day is fixed. The marriage cannot take place unless the man and the woman accept each other. The man's family must also give a 'mahr' (wedding gift) to his bride-to-be. The value of this is not laid down and depends on the circumstances of the two families.

A Muslim wedding

A Muslim wedding is a very simple affair. The most important part is the signing of a formal contract between the bridegroom and the bride's male guardian in front of two male Muslims. The contract usually lays down a specific sum of money for the mahr, which comes from the bridegroom's family to the bride and remains her personal possession in case the couple should divorce.

A Muslim wedding can take place anywhere since it is essentially a civil rather than a religious ceremony. In Britain it is usually, however, performed by an imam in a mosque. He will open the ceremony by reading from the Qur'an – usually from the fourth sura, which is entitled 'The Woman'. The imam then talks about marriage and the responsibilities that the man and the woman have towards each other. The couple then exchange rings. The ring placed on the man's finger must not be made of gold. Guests congratulate the couple saying:

Baarakal-lahu lakum wa baraka 'alaikum.
(May God bless you and invoke his benediction upon you.)

A feast follows, sometimes with singing and dancing.

What does marriage mean to Muslims?

Work to do

1. Asked about arranged marriages, a young Muslim replied:
   When you think about it, marriage is much more than the joining together of a man and a woman. Amongst Muslims it brings together and unites two families and so a large number of people are involved. Also, as young people, we need to draw on the wisdom of those older than us before making such an important decision. That is why divorce is very rare in Muslim societies.
   (a) Do you think that there is something to be said for arranged marriages?
   (b) What are the main arguments for and against arranged marriages?

2. The Qur'an says:
   If you cannot deal equitably and justly with more than one wife, you shall marry only one.
   (a) What is polygamy?
   (b) How many wives does the Qur'an allow a Muslim man to have?
   (c) How many husbands does the Qur'an allow a Muslim woman to have?
   (d) Under what kind of circumstances might a Muslim man consider polygamy today?

3. A tradition going back to Muhammad teaches that 'marriage is half religion'. What do you think is meant by this statement?

Key words **arranged marriage:** one in which the negotiations for a marriage are carried out by members of the families of the couple to be married

Two male witnesses are required at every Muslim wedding. Why do you think witnesses are thought to be so important?

17.3 The place of women in Islam

Focusing questions

- What are the different rules in Muslim society for men owning property and women owning property?
- What rules does the Qur'an lay down for women's dress?
- What does the Qur'an expect a man to do for his family and what is the woman's main responsibility?

The Qur'an teaches that all men and women are the children of Adam and Eve (the first man and woman) and so are equal in God's sight. Allah has, however, given them different tasks to perform and different roles to play. The Qur'an and Muslim tradition have much to say about the role women should play in family life and in society generally:

☐ From the time of Muhammad, Muslim women have had the right to own property in their own name and to dispose of it as they wish. They also have the right to share in the wealth of their dead relatives, although they receive only half as much as a similarly placed man would receive. The reason for this discrepancy between the sexes is that Muslim men are responsible for looking after their family, including their female relatives. Females, however, are not responsible for their male relatives.

☐ The Qur'an insists that all women should dress modestly and behave decently in public. In many Muslim countries women wear the traditional long dress and head veil. Dressing in this way is called **hijab**.

An African Muslim with her children.

The restrictions about female dress have been interpreted differently in different countries. In Iran, for example, since the Muslim revolution in 1979 women have worn the 'chador' – a long black gown. In Indonesia, and some other Muslim countries, rules about dress are much more relaxed.

☐ Women may attend the mosque but they have their own separate washing and prayer facilities. There is a distinction between the responsibilities of men and those of women in this respect. Whilst Muslim men are expected to attend the mosque frequently – especially at noon on Friday – women must always put the demands of their families first.

Women at work

Muslim women are allowed to work outside the home as long as it does not interfere with their domestic responsibilities. In most Muslim countries women tend to work in the 'caring' professions – social work, medicine and teaching.

Key question **What rights and responsibilities do women have in Islam?**

From the Qur'an

Tell the believing men to lower their gaze and be chaste; that is purer for them: lo! God is aware of what they do. And tell the believing women to lower their gaze and be chaste and to display of their adornment only that which is apparent, and to draw their headcoverings over their breasts.

☐ How does this verse tell men and women to behave towards members of the opposite sex?

Work to do

1. Muhammad told his followers:
  Modesty is part of faith.'
Why do you think Muhammad considered dress and religious faith to be so closely linked?

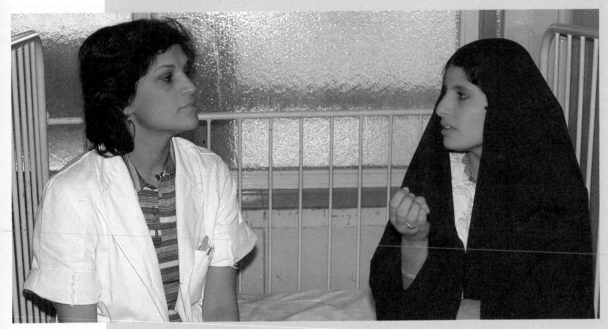

A doctor and patient in Kuwait.

2. Look at this photograph of two Muslim women. One is dressed traditionally, while the other (a doctor) is dressed more like a Westerner. Do you think that from a Muslim point of view there is a danger when some Muslims begin to adopt Western ways of behaving? If so, what might those dangers be?

Key words **hijab:** literally 'veil', now refers to the practice of requiring women to keep their bodies and faces covered

17.4 Divorce

Focusing questions:
■ How does Islam treat adultery?
■ How does a Muslim man obtain a divorce?
■ How does Islam seek to safeguard the rights of women?

Marriage is the corner-stone of every Muslim society, placing heavy obligations upon all those who marry. The break-up of a marriage is not only a tragedy for the two people concerned but also for their families. However, Muslims do recognise that there is no value in keeping a marriage going when the union has no future.

Divorce, therefore, is reluctantly allowed in Muslim societies. It should, however, never be undertaken lightly, as the two quotations from the Hadith opposite make clear.

Conditions for divorce

Before the birth of Islam, men in Arabia were able to discard their wife at any time. To stop this happening, and to safeguard the rights of women, Islam laid down several conditions for divorce:

☐ There must be a compulsory interval of four months between a man saying that he wants a divorce and the event itself taking place. This allows an attempt to be made at reconciliation.
☐ If a woman is pregnant then the husband must support her until the baby is born.
☐ A divorced woman must be allowed to keep the dowry that was given to her when she married, as well as the contents of her home. After a divorce has been granted it is the responsibility of the woman's male relatives to support her, although her former husband is still financially responsible for his children.

Under Muslim law, once a man has divorced his wife he is not allowed to remarry her unless she has remarried and either divorced her second husband or become a widow. Even then there must be a gap of at least four months after the death or divorce to make sure that the woman is not pregnant by her previous husband.

Obtaining a divorce

It is easy for a man to obtain a divorce in a Muslim society. He must announce on three separate occasions that he wishes to divorce his wife. A clear month must elapse between the first two of these statements. During this time the couple must live together in the same house without there being any physical contact between them. Should any contact take place, then the divorce cannot go ahead and the marriage continues unbroken.

Adultery

It is well-known that the crime of adultery is treated with the greatest severity in Muslim countries. The penalty laid down in the Qur'an is that both the man and the woman should receive in public 100 lashes from a whip. In a few strict Muslim countries couples are put to death for committing adultery.

On what basis is divorce allowed in a Muslim society?

Extracts from the Hadith on divorce

(a) *Allah's messenger, Muhammad, said: 'The most hated thing which is allowed by Allah is divorce.'*
(b) *The Prophet Muhammad said: 'Marry and do not divorce, for the throne of Allah is shaken when divorce happens.'*

☐ On the basis of these two quotations, and the text, how would you sum up the attitude of Islam towards divorce?

Work to do
1. Why do you think that a period of four months is set aside for a couple to try to solve their problems? What might
   (a) the husband
   (b) the wife
   (c) any children
gain from this period?

2. Concerning divorce, the Qur'an says:
   If ye fear a breach
   Between the two of them,
   Appoint 'two' arbiters,
   One from his family,
   And the other from hers;
   If they wish for peace,
   God will cause
   Their reconciliation:
   For God hath full knowledge:
   And is acquainted
   With all things.
   (a) How does this extract from the Qur'an suggest that a breach between a husband and a wife can be healed?
   (b) If the couple desire peace, who is it that will bring about their reconciliation?

3. Why do you think that the penalties for adultery are so severe in Muslim societies? What, do you think, is there about adultery that Muslims see as being particularly dangerous?

17.5 Food

Focusing questions

- Why does the Qur'an lay down certain stipulations about food and drink?
- Which is the animal whose meat Muslims are forbidden to eat?
- What is halal and what are the main rules covering the slaughter of animals?

The overwhelming majority of foods are lawful in Islam. Eating, with thankfulness, the pure and wholesome foods that Allah has given is, in itself, an act of worship. In Islam a moderate and healthy diet is as much a religious responsibility as it is necessary for the physical, mental and moral health of the individual and society. There are, however, a few forbidden foods and drinks.

Forbidden food

According to the Qur'an a Muslim must not eat or drink:

- meat whose method of slaughter is unknown or which still contains the blood of the animal;
- pigs since these animals are renowned for their filth, living, as they do, off rotting foods and offal – they are also very prone to disease and their meat is very fatty;
- any animal which has been killed in any other name than Allah's;
- alcohol ('intoxicants').

Obviously, if the choice is between starvation and eating forbidden foods, then the believer should eat. The laws, however, have been laid down by Allah to protect the health and well-being of the Muslim community and as such should be welcomed. In laying down these laws Allah is seeking to protect the minds and bodies of all Muslims.

Even lawful food has to be killed according to certain strict conditions (halal) before it is suitable for a Muslim to eat (see 16.3). Every effort should be made to slaughter an animal with compassion. This is done by slitting the throat with a knife that is as sharp as possible so that the animal's death is quick and relatively painless. The animal should not see the knife nor should it have its death witnessed by another animal. It should be transported comfortably to the place of slaughter and left free to toss about as it bleeds.

Alcohol

According to the Qur'an the date-palm and vine provide fresh fruits, date-honey and vinegar. Yet from rotted, fermented fruits come the intoxicants which destabilise individuals and communities. Allah has provided everything in nature for us to enjoy but he allows Satan to try and lure us from the straight way through a misuse of his gifts. Alcohol is one such misuse.

Key question Why are Muslims forbidden to eat certain foods and to drink alcohol?

The Qur'an on forbidden food

> He hath only forbidden you,
> Dead meat and blood,

And the flesh of swine,
And that on which
Any other name hath been invoked
Besides that of God . . .
O ye who believe!
Intoxicants and gambling . . .
Are an abomination –
Of Satan's handiwork.

☐ In this extract six different things are forbidden for the Muslim. What are they?
☐ Who is Satan?

For He commands them
What is just and forbids them
What is evil; He allows
Them as lawful what is good
'And pure' and prohibits them
From what is bad 'and impure'.

☐ How does this extract suggest that anything forbidden to the Muslims is only forbidden for their own good?

Work to do

1. In the Hadith we read of a man who came to stay with the Prophet Muhammad and brought a large bottle of wine with him as a gift.

The Prophet Muhammad said, 'Didn't you know that Allah has prohibited it?'

Then the man said, 'Shall I sell it?'

The Prophet Muhammad said, 'He who prohibited it prohibited selling it.'

The man said, 'Should I give it as a gift to the Jews?'

The Prophet Muhammad said, 'He who prohibited it prohibited giving it as a gift.'

The man said, 'What shall I do with it then?'

The Prophet Muhammad said, 'Throw it away.'

(a) How would you sum up the Muslim attitude to alcohol?

(b) Why is Islam so strongly opposed to alcohol?

2. Imagine a Muslim family of father, mother, two teenage children and one young child aged seven. They are living in this country. What problems do you think that each member of this family might have in keeping to the Muslim food and drink laws whilst living a normal life in Britain?

17.6 Death and burial

Focusing questions

■ What do Muslims try to do to prepare themselves for death?
■ How is the body treated after death?
■ What period is set aside for mourning in a Muslim community?

It was reported that Muhammad prayed as he was dying:

Allah, help me through the hardship and agony of death.

He also asked for the forgiveness of his sins. Muslims try to face the end of their lives by following Muhammad's example. They believe strongly in the resurrection of the body and in a life after death, so they try to face death without fear and in a spirit of hope. After death the soul enters into eternal life and is reunited with departed friends.

Approaching death

With death approaching, Muslims hope that they will be able to recite the Shahada before departing from this life so that their sins may be forgiven by Allah. Relatives and friends gather around the dying person's bedside to read from the Qur'an and say prayers. They ask that Allah will be merciful to the soul of the person about to die.

After death

After death the corpse is washed in scented water by a member of the same sex and dressed in white robes. A male is dressed in three robes and a female in five. If the person has been on the pilgrimage to Makka they may have brought back with them the sheets which they wore, which have been washed in the waters of the holy well at Zam-Zam. If so, their body will be wrapped in them. An important principle is that, in death, rich and poor are treated in exactly the same way since all are equal in God's sight. The body is taken to the mosque or an open space for the funeral prayer. This can be led either by the imam or by a member of the family. The funeral prayer contains the words:

O God, pardon this dead person; lo, Thou art the Most Forgiving, the Most Merciful.

Following this the body is taken into the cemetery to be buried. Muslims never cremate their dead. In Muslim countries a coffin is not used – the grave is therefore dug to fit the size of the body. Muslims believe that it is very important for the body to be in actual contact with the earth. After more prayers have been said the body is laid in the grave with the right side facing Makka and the head turned in that direction as well.

Mourning

The Prophet Muhammad wept when his son died and Muslims do not need to feel ashamed at weeping either. They do find the thought that the soul has returned to the God who made it comforting. The period of mourning can last for any length of time between seven days and three months. After burial it is believed that the grave is visited by two angels who question the dead person about their fitness for the next life and for the Day of Judgement.

Key question **What do Muslims believe about life after death and how do these beliefs affect the way that they deal with death itself?**

An extract from the Qur'an concerning death

> *In the name of God*
> *We commit to the earth, according to the way of the Prophet God . . .*
> *We created you from it, and return you into it,*
> *and from it We will raise you a second time.*

☐ Who is 'We' in this passage?
☐ When will the people be raised from the earth a second time?

A Muslim funeral. Why do Muslims not use a coffin?

Work to do
Muslims believe that after a person has died two angels visit the grave in order to examine the dead person's fitness for the Day of Judgement. It is fitting, therefore, that mourners should try to prompt the person as to the answers that they give the angels:

> *O male or female servant of God, remember the covenant made while leaving the world, that is the attestation that there is no God if not God Himself, and that Muhammad is the Messenger of God, and the belief that paradise is a verity, that hell is a verity, that the questioning in the grave is a verity, that the Day of Judgement shall come, there being no doubt about it – that God will resuscitate those who are in graves, that thou hast accepted God as thy Lord, Islam as thy religion, Muhammad as thy prophet, the Qur'an as thy guide, the Ka'ba as thy direction to turn to for the service of worship and that all believers are thy brethren. May God keep thee firm in this trial.*

(a) What is a 'verity'? How many such verities are mentioned here?

(b) There are several signs in this extract of the true Muslim, who can look forward to the Day of Judgement with confidence. What are they?

KEY WORDS

The unit number tells you where to find the explanations.

hajj 15.6
halal 16.3
hallot 3.1
Hannukah 3.4
haram 16.3
Havdalah 3.1
Hebrew 1.1
Hebrews 1.1
heretic 6.5
heresy 8.2
Herod the Great 1.4
Herzl 1.7
hijab 17.3
hijra 12.3
Holocaust 1.6
Holy Spirit 6.3
host 10.5

I Iblis 14.2
icon 7.2
ihram 15.6
imam 12.5
Incarnation 6.3
Inquisition 6.5
Isaac 1.2
Israel 1.1
Israelites 1.1

J Jacob 1.2
Jesus Christ 6.1
Jews 1.1
Jewish Bible 1.2
jihad 12.4
Judah 1.4
Judaism 1.1

K Ka'ba 12.2
ketubah 5.4
Kiddush 3.1
kingdom of God 6.2
kosher 4.3

L Lent 10.2
Liturgy 7.2
Lord's Prayer 9.5
Luke 6.4
lunar year 12.3
Luther 1.5

M Madina 12.2
Mahdi 12.5

Makka 12.2
Mass 7.3
matrimony 11.1
Maundy Thursday 10.3
meditation 9.5
menorah 3.4
Messiah 2.1
Methodism 7.5
mezuzah 4.2
midrash 5.1
mihrab 15.2
minaret 16.1
minister 9.1
misbaha 14.1
mitzvot 5.2
mohel 4.3
mosque 12.3
muezzin 16.1
Muhammad 12.1

N neo-Orthodoxy 1.8
Ner Tamid 4.1
New Testament 8.2
Nicene Creed 6.3
non-Orthodox Jews 1.8
Nonconformist 7.1

O Old Testament 8.3
Orthodox Church 6.1
Orthodox Jews 1.8

P parable 6.2
paschal 10.4
Passion Sunday 10.3
patriarchs 1.2
Patrick 6.5
Paul 6.4
Pentateuch 2.3
Pentecost 6.4
Pentecostal movement 9.1
Pesach 1.3
Peter 6.4
Philistines 1.4
Pontius Pilate 6.2
Pope 7.1
Presbyterians 7.5
priest 6.1
prophet 12.1
Protestant Church 6.1
pulpit 9.3

purgatory 11.6
Purim 3.5

Q qibla 15.2
Quakers 6.1
Qur'an 12.1

R rabbi 4.3
rak'a 15.3
Ramadan 15.5
Resurrection 10.4
Roman Catholic Church 6.1
rosary 9.5
Rosh Hashanah 3.2
Ruth 3.7

S sacrament 7.3
sadaqa 15.4
salat 15.2
Salvation Army 6.1
Satan 14.2
scribe 4.3
Second Vatican Council 6.5
seder 3.6
Sefer Torah 2.3
shabat 2.3
Shahada 12.2
Shari'a 12.5
Shavuot 3.3
Shechita 4.3
Shema 2.1
shochet 4.3
shofar 3.2

Siddur 2.4
Simhat Torah 3.3
speaking in tongues 9.1
Star of David 4.1
Sukkot 3.3
Sunna 13.2
synagogue 1.5
Synoptic Gospels 8.3

T tallit 4.2
Talmud 2.1
Tawhid 14.1
tefillin 4.2
The Ten Sayings 1.3
Torah 1.2
transfiguration 10.2
transubstantiation 9.2
Trinity 6.3
Trinity Sunday 10.5

V Virgin Birth 6.3
Virgin Mary 7.3

W Whit Sunday 10.5
World Council of Churches 6.5

Y yad 2.3
yarmulka 4.2
Yom Kippur 3.2

Z zakat 15.4
Zealots 1.4
Zeus 3.4
Zionist 1.7